MW01046281

No Path But My Own

No Path But My Own

Horseback Adventures
in the Chilcotin
and the Rockies

Cliff Kopas
Leslie Kopas

HARBOUR PUBLISHING

Copyright © 1996 Leslie Kopas

All rights reserved. No part of this book may be reproduced in any form by any means without the written permission of the publisher; except by a reviewer, who may quote passages in a review.

Harbour Publishing
Box 219
Madeira Park, BC V0N 2H0

Edited by Susan Mayse.
All photographs from the Cliff Kopas collection.
Map design by Bob Harris. Maps by Fiona MacGregor.
Cover painting by Diana Durrand.
Cover design by Roger Handling, Terra Firma.
Page design & layout by David Lee Communications.

Published with the assistance of the Canada Council and the Cultural Services Branch of the BC Ministry of Tourism and Ministry Responsible for Culture.
Printed and bound in Canada.

Canadian Cataloguing in Publication Data

Kopas, Cliff, 1911–1978
  No path but my own

Includes index.
ISBN 1-55017-151-8

  1. Kopas, Cliff, 1911–1978. 2. Pack transportation—British Columbia. 3. Pack-horse camping—British Columbia. 4. British Columbia—Description and travel. I. Kopas, Leslie. II. Title.
FC3817.3.K662 1996   917.1104'3   C96-910511-8
F1087.K662 1996

Contents

FOREWORD

When I was a youngster I believed that my father had been born at the age of twenty-one. He did not speak of an earlier time in his life. His talk was of his salad days, his packhorse trips into the Rocky Mountains and the plateau above our home at Bella Coola.

His trips took place in the 1930s, an unfathomably remote time to a child in the 1940s. Some of his trail companions lived in Bella Coola but they were old, perhaps thirty-six. I could not imagine these men on trips; they seemed to work all the time like my father.

Another element of my father's stories appeared in Bella Coola on horseback every summer: Carrier Indians from Ulkatcho and Anahim Lake. They were exceedingly exotic. I rented my bicycle to them for fifty cents an hour and spoke broken English even though they may have understood me perfectly anyway. I intended to learn to speak Carrier but never got around to it.

Years passed. Eventually my father's collection of excellent photographs became mine. They were haphazardly organized, stuffed in bunches into ordinary envelopes and cursorily documented. My father had lived a busy life running a retail store, writing magazine articles and books, raising four children and throwing himself into community projects. Filing photographic negatives was a chore that could be postponed—and was.

I had absorbed my father's interest in photography. Organizing his negative collection was no burden to me. I spent happy days in the darkroom watching old times come alive in the developer.

I thumbed through the photographic file sheets often. They were entertaining; they told picture stories—stories that I had heard long ago in words. They told of a time when Indians rode horses rather than pickup trucks, a time before a barrier of park permits, restrictions, regulations and prohibitions had been placed over the southern Rockies, a time when a doctor had the time to ride horseback for three weeks to see a handful of Stick Indian patients, pulling teeth under the jackpines like a demented dentist.

There was also an unpublished manuscript. It was apparent that the photographs and manuscript belonged together; they told the same stories. In my estimation the manuscript was too earnest for the adventures it related. These were campfire stories. They had their truths to tell but they needed embellishment.

To hold to the truth, I researched. I joined a packhorse expedition across Spatsizi Plateau in northern British Columbia and learned that packhorsing is very hard work. The guide told me that his horses were sweeties, but sometimes they exasperated him so much that he felt like gut-shooting the bunch and watching them die. Next I went to the Rocky Mountains—no horses admitted unless accompanied by a responsible park warden. With a fistful of campground permits I backpacked the trails of Yoho, Kootenay, Banff, Assiniboine and Kananaskis, then spilled out onto the prairies at Sheep Creek. Closer to home I walked from Anahim Lake to Ulkatcho, stopping on the way at Salmon River to meet Joe Cahoose, who had guided my father to Tetachuck Lake in 1938. I had cunningly brought my father's photographs with me. Mary Cahoose, Joe's wife, identified faces half a century old. I camped beside the spirit houses in the abandoned Ulkatcho village, then climbed into the Rainbow Mountains. I met nobody in a week except moose, bears, caribou and wolf. (The wolf was pursuing the caribou, which escaped.) I trudged up and down Tweedsmuir Trail, Burnt Bridge Trail, Capoose Trail and Canoe Crossing Trail. Truth to tell, the research was an excuse to travel the country. It was wonderfully satisfying.

Eventually I felt informed enough to tackle the manuscript. I added some dialogue. The photographs held me to the veracity of the stories.

In his book *Klondike*, Pierre Berton remarked that most of the men in the Yukon gold rush were in their twenties, young enough to be foolhardy, optimistic and carefree: a good description of Cliff Kopas. In climbing the Chilkoot Pass the goldrushers learned that they were capable of overcoming great obstacles; they lived the rest of their lives confidently, as though they were scaling a perpetual Chilkoot Pass. Cliff Kopas scaled his Chilkoot Pass by overcoming polio to make his audacious journeys into our western mountains and plateaus.

—*Leslie Kopas*

Cliff Kopas at his portable typewriter in a cabin near Anahim Lake, 1937.

PRELUDE:
A PRESCRIPTION OF MOUNTAINS

"For I carry my antidotes within myself, which are resolution
and patience."   Michel de Montaigne, *Essays*

The Kopas farm near Okotoks, Alberta.

THE ROCKY MOUNTAINS COMMANDED the western horizon of my boyhood. They were a jagged wall which advanced to glisten in the morning sun, then retreated behind evening shadows with only saw teeth showing. In winter a chinook arch glowed above them, breathing warm air onto the prairies, removing the snow. From the Rockies came the water which rippled over the old Sheep Creek ford at Okotoks near my school.

The mountains were fascinating, spellbinding. They were like gods: unchangeable yet changing, known about by everyone yet known to few, always there yet nigh inaccessible. For me, at least. The wheat farmers of Okotoks had no interest in mountains. My father said, "Too steep to plough."

The schoolteacher at Okotoks introduced me to books about the fur traders and railway surveyors who had known the mountains. These men showed the Rockies not as an impenetrable wall but as a region of valleys and passes. I wanted to go where they had gone, to the heart of the mountains.

I was fourteen years old in 1925. I had not yet been to the mountains but I was almost independent enough to reach them on my own. Before I had the chance, I became very ill.

I fell into bed with a high fever, a severe headache and pain in my neck, arms and legs. My muscles were extremely tender. I felt terribly weak. In a few days I could not move my legs.

The doctor came. He told my mother, "Your son has polio. It is a severe case. He may not walk again."

Despair swept through me. The tears I wept brought no relief. My muscles were so badly paralyzed that they threatened to deform my still-growing bones. The doctor operated several times.

After each operation I asked, "Will I be able to walk now?"

The doctor always said, "I hope so." Finally he told me, "The polio infection is gone now, although the paralysis remains. You can expect some improvement. Your recovery will depend greatly on your determination and courage."

The doctor set my legs in casts where they remained for many months. Several gifts helped to fill the long days of convalescence.

A pair of field glasses brought the Rockies closer. I scanned the mountains every day, noting the quick arrival of snow in autumn and its reluctant departure in spring. An immense topographical map with a scale of three miles to the inch showed me the valleys and passes from Okotoks to Lake Windermere in British Columbia. A network of dotted lines signified trails. The Rockies were laid out on my bed, rising from my paralyzed legs. In my imagination I travelled their trails.

My imaginary travels were given a realistic setting when I received a *National Geographic* magazine containing sixty photographs by the Banff photographer Byron Harmon. He had taken a five-hundred-mile expedition with packhorses through the Rockies with the sole purpose of getting pictures. The grandeur of the scenes and the adventure of packhorse travel set my imagination aflame, and the story released me from despair. I perceived that even a lame person can ride a horse.

Hard on the heels of Byron Harmon's photographs came a book by J. Monroe Thorington. Vivid stories of first ascents and magnificent photographs of mountains and packtrains lifted me from my bed. I flew to high camps; I helped Thorington's wrangler, Ulysse La Casse, across the Saskatchewan Glacier with a string of packhorses.

I could not live outdoors, so I lived in outdoor books. The cowboy author Will James became my model. I wanted to emulate his approach to life: a love of freedom and horses, a disdain for hardship and danger, a life of courage and good humour.

Eventually the doctor removed the casts from my legs and said, "I have done what I can. The rest of it is up to you. Your leg muscles have been permanently impaired; you will be lame for the rest of your life. But your muscles will not deteriorate further. Use them hard. Be tough and brave, like an explorer."

In my mind's eye, I was still the same boy who once ran everywhere, swam in Sheep Creek and shinnied up cottonwood trees. I stood up—and I fell.

To walk, just to walk, however haltingly, was my aim. When

finally I achieved it, I vowed never to think of myself as a handicapped person, never to speak of my disability and never to use it as an excuse. I was in good health; the residual paralysis was only a nuisance.

For some time I could not walk the mile and a half to school at Okotoks. My parents bought Dick, a brown Standardbred gelding, for me to ride. Dick was a magnificent animal: tall, gentle, patient and wise. I was immensely proud of him.

Dick put me within range of the Okotoks school. He also put me within range of the Rocky Mountains.

First Trails in the Rockies and Purcells

"He surely wanted nothing from the wilderness but space to breathe in and to push on through. His need was to exist, and to move onwards at the greatest possible risk, and maximum of privation."
Joseph Conrad,
Heart of Darkness

The west side of North Kananaskis Pass.

15

ROCKY MOUNTAINS TRIP 1932

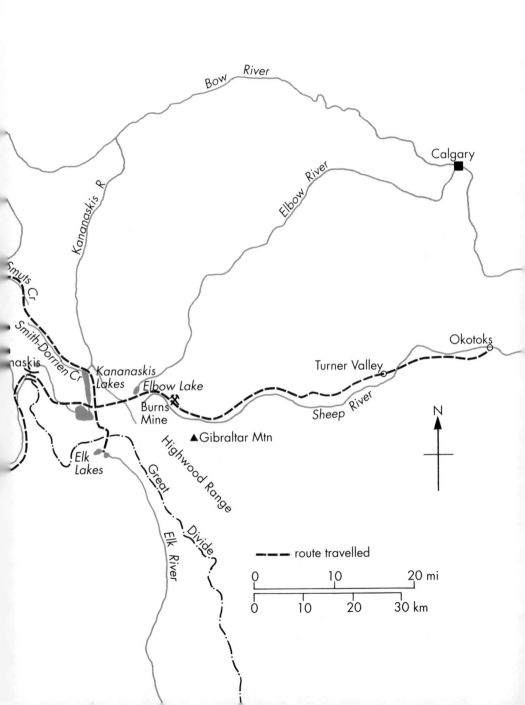

Bow River

Calgary

Kananaskis R

Elbow River

Smuts Cr.

Smith-Dorrien Cr

...naskis

Kananaskis
Lakes

Elbow Lake

Okotoks

Turner Valley

Burns
Mine

Sheep River

▲Gibraltar Mtn

N

Elk
Lakes

Highwood Range

Great

Divide

Elk River

- - - route travelled

0   10   20 mi

0   10   20   30 km

Early on the last day of June, the sun peered over the edge of the prairie and suffused the world with gold.

Into this golden world walked Neil Mackay and I, Neil intent on horses and I admiring the sunrise. The colours of dawn soon disappeared, as had one of our horses. It was Rex. The sly old devil had found a soft place in the fence.

"That horse has no more sense than a little kid with a big belly button," growled Neil.

"For a short-sighted animal he surely has a keen eye for weakness in a fence," I said.

Already annoyed by Rex, Neil was further annoyed by my bookish talk. "Cut the tail off that word 'surely,'" he snorted. "When we are packhorsing it will make us sound like dude kids still in school."

"It would be pretty close to the truth," I pointed out.

The five horses that had not strayed scarcely looked up as we approached. Neil put a halter on Jimmy; I did the same to Dick. While I drove the three loose horses back toward the corral, Neil set off in search of Rex.

I had hardly closed the corral gate when Neil returned, driving Rex ahead of him.

"Where was he?" I asked.

"In the hollow picking the neighbour's oats. It is a good thing we are heading for the hills. We will escape the posse."

"In Alberta it will be the Royal Canadian Mounted Police," I said, faithful to western Canadian history.

"For that pathetic patch of oats, it probably won't be anyone. The soil is so dry the oat stalks were following the dog around."

The land was indeed dry. On the flatlands of southwestern Alberta rain was as scarce as paid work. Neil and I had discussed the predicament of being young men in a place that had no need for our energy and ambitions.

"We was calved at the wrong time and place," said Neil in resignation.

I had other thoughts, born of stories of people who had moved

18

west across Canada. "The way I see it, we are free," I said. "We aren't trapped here like the farmers. We can go."

"Then let's go somewheres we don't have to prime ourselves to spit."

The Rocky Mountains promised to fulfil some of our dreams. Neil wanted to be a horseman; I wanted to be an explorer. We were at last old enough to travel and we were not expected to work, since there was no work.

Besides our saddlehorses, Jimmy and Dick, we had two fillies given to us free for the breaking by someone who may not have been a friend. The young horses did not have names; we decided to name them after we got to know them. To round out our outfit, we had two experienced packhorses named Rex and Kit.

"I'm a little worried about packing the young ones," I admitted to Neil. "We are pretty green at this."

"So are they," Neil replied airily. "That makes us even."

Cliff Kopas with Dick and Rex in the Rockies.

We took off our boots at the farm house door and entered the kitchen, greeted by a chorus of "mornings" from my parents and Sheldon, my older brother.

"Help yourselves to coffee. How many eggs do you boys want?" asked my mother.

"Eat lots," my father advised. "It will be the last good meal you will have for six weeks."

"I bet it will be more like six hours," said Sheldon. "They will still be trying to pack the unbroke horses this afternoon, and then it will be time for supper."

Neil's parents arrived at six-thirty with a formidable pile of provisions. I looked at Neil accusingly. "We have only four packhorses."

"It's my parents," he said with a shrug. "They are sure we are going to get lost in the mountains."

Neil would have been appalled if he had known that I hoped his parents were right. The early explorers had done a lot of starving. I wanted some privation; I believed it would make our experience more authentic.

Remarking that he was fascinated by scenes of disaster, Sheldon accompanied Neil and me to the corral.

The two unbroke horses were very different in appearance. One was a plump little animal with warm brown eyes, the other a sinister-looking creature with one grey eye and one brown eye.

Neil suggested, "Let's try the one with the two-tone eyes first."

I handed Sheldon the halter rope. "Your job, brother." I placed a saddle blanket on the malicious-looking horse's back. It quivered. I set the packsaddle on top of the blanket, and Neil pulled the breeching over the animal's hindquarters. At that the horse burst into action. Her head went down and her back went up. The packsaddle and blanket landed on the ground. Sheldon spun around on the end of the halter rope, then let go. The horse stopped immediately and stared at us.

"She seems offended by the breeching," I said.

"A little education never hurt nobody, and accepting breeching is part of a packhorse's education," declared Neil.

"When it comes to education, you two don't have enough of it to read the writing on the wall," said Sheldon. "You need help."

He was proved right; the second lesson was as unsuccessful as the first.

"Without a thorough revision of her attitude toward breeching, this horse is going to delay us indefinitely," I observed.

"We don't need breeching until we reach steep country," Neil said. "After the fillies get used to their packs, they will accept the breeching."

"How do you know they will accept the packs?" Sheldon asked sceptically.

Neil and Sheldon saddled the packhorses easily without the breeching. I kept a close eye on them while I filled packboxes.

"I've read that horses puff up when they are first saddled," I asserted.

"Listen to the library cowboy," grinned Neil, feeling superior now that he had successfully saddled our horses. "I once seen him get throwed by a three-legged stool in the school library."

The sun was getting high and hot by the time we had filled the four pairs of packboxes and balanced each pair for weight. We led the brown-eyed filly to the nearest pair of packboxes. We set the packboxes in the basket ropes and snugged them tight. Before we could tie the hitches, the horse bucked—just once but it was enough. The packboxes and their contents reached the ground with a crash.

"Just the disaster I came to see," exclaimed Sheldon. "I'll go get the truck. It won't buck your packboxes off."

We loaded our grub and gear into the back of the truck. Then Sheldon slid behind the wheel and headed west to Bob Carey's ranch west of Turner Valley. Neil and I followed on our saddlehorses, leading the two young horses and driving the other two packhorses ahead of us.

"The fillies will be well halter-broke by the end of the day and trail broke too," said Neil. "Bob Carey is a good packer. He will educate them to packs for us."

"And educate us too," I added humbly. I feared that the young horses were too wild for us to handle and that our trip would end before it even started.

We reached Bob Carey's place at dusk. As soon as we had unloaded our gear from the truck, Sheldon started back to Okotoks.

Bob Carey said, "You boys look plumb tuckered. I bet your tapeworms are hollering for food. I happen to have some bacon and eggs handy."

A young cowboy named Tommy Livingston drifted in, apparently lured by bacon-scented air. He asked Bob about work on the ranch. "The only position open on this outfit is for rain-maker," said Bob. "But at this precise moment we need someone to help finish up these bacon and eggs. How do you like your eggs, staring at you or blinded?"

The clatter of stove lids woke us in the morning.

"You boys going to sleep all day?" asked Bob Carey. "The sun is stretching, ready to get up; that's what you should do too. Riding in the cool of the day will save your horses."

I felt miserable. My legs had cramped in the night as the doctor had warned me they would from time to time. My hip and shoulder bones had fought the floor all night and lost. My neck was aflame with sunburn. I was also very saddlesore.

Tommy Livingston livened the morning with profane wit, enlarging my vocabulary without enriching it. After he had left to continue his search for work or another meal, I asked Bob, "Do all cowboys swear as bad as Tommy?"

"No, some are good at it," Bob replied.

After breakfast Bob Carey taught Neil and me how to pack a horse. We saddled Rex and practised the diamond hitch over empty packboxes until the horse groaned with impatience. As a horseman, Bob was as much concerned about imparting to us the proper attitude toward horses as he was about packing. He exhorted us, "A horseman never mistreats a horse. They aren't pets but they deserve respect. Take care of their backs and bellies—don't sore them or let them go gaunt— and they will take you where you want to go."

The two young horses seemed to sense that an experienced person was working with them. After a little dancing about, they accepted the breeching. They stood still while the packboxes were hitched to the packsaddle; they shifted only a little to brace themselves as the lash rope was pulled tight to make the diamond on top of the load.

Bob Carey educated Neil and me in courage, too, through the example of his life. In 1916 he had been in the Battle of the Somme in France. On his first charge over the top of the trench he was hit above the left knee. He made a tourniquet of his puttee to stop the bleeding and then cut off his own shattered lower leg. After twenty-five hours he was rescued and moved to England. He underwent seventeen amputations for gangrene which was stopped four inches from his hip joint. He returned to western Alberta with an artificial leg to resume his cowboy life. He ran cattle on the Forest Reserve for the Sheep Creek Stock Association. He was a superb horseman and continued to ride the rough ones.

It was near noon before we were ready to pull out. Bob Carey hobbled to the gate and let our six-horse string pass through. "Keep a close eye on those packs—and good luck, boys."

"We can't thank you enough, Bob."

"Come back with six horses in good shape and I will consider myself thanked."

Neil and I turned toward the mountains. A dirt road bordered by wild roses led into the Forest Reserve, winding first among hills, then between the outliers of the Rocky Mountains.

I was in the lead on Dick. He was keen for new sights and sounds, his ears forward. I led the soft-eyed filly while Neil, at the rear, led the one with the eyes of different colours. Between us were Rex and Kit, travelling free, snatching mouthfuls of grass as they went.

We stopped at the Forest Reserve ranger station to ask about the trail to Kananaskis Lakes and beyond. A packtrain outfitter named Geddic was visiting the ranger. The two men vied for the most uncomplimentary description of the trails.

23

"Whose job is it to repair them?" I hazarded.

"The government's—but the government is broke," answered the ranger quickly.

"I didn't expect hard times in the mountains," I said.

"It's hard times everywhere," remarked Geddic. He paused. "By the look of your outfit you aren't suffering none. You should see the poor tramps I come acrost trying to stay alive by fishing and poaching. It's always too tough for 'em in the mountains and they head back to the city even worse off." He looked at our packhorses with an expert eye. "You boys sure done a good job of packing."

"We've never had a pack turn on us or had a sore back," Neil bragged.

"I'm mighty impressed. Hardly any horseman can admit that with a straight face," replied Geddic with a flicker of a smile. "You must of worked into the horse business gradual-like. You sit in the saddle like you never rode much; at the same time you are top-notch packers. You must of just got to the point where you can afford saddlehorses. Did you lead your packhorses on foot before?"

"That's right," affirmed Neil, stung by the implication that we rode like dudes. "Times have been tough for us too."

"I'm going through to Kananaskis in a few days myself," said Geddic. "If you are still there, you can show me the fine points of packing—and we can tell a few tall stories."

Late in the afternoon we reached Indian Oils, a small coal mine at the end of the road. A man stepped onto the porch of one of the shacks. "Best stop here for the night, boys," he said. "You can put your horses in with Geddic's bunch in the pasture. It's quite a ways to the next good grass."

Buck, the coal miner, invited us to spend the night in his shack. His two partners had gone to town for a few days. After supper he took us to his mine, a shaft of steam coal some twenty feet thick. On our way back to the shack a thunderstorm swept over the mountains. The miner rushed back to his shack. Neil and I turned our faces to the rain and let it stream over us.

In the morning Buck helped us pack. Residing at the beginning of the trail, he had observed many outfits saddle up and start into the mountains. But, like Neil and me, he lacked precision in his knowledge of packing.

The brown-eyed filly accepted her pack with scarcely a quiver. The one with the unmatched eyes was still rebellious. For a start she bucked off her saddle blanket.

"If we can't get the saddle blanket on, we are a long way from the diamond hitch," I said despondently.

Buck suggested, "She might gentle down if we put a blindfold on her." He had seen it done before.

It was bad advice, and we took it.

I put a gunny sack over the filly's eyes and tucked it through her halter. Then I held the halter tight while Neil and Buck put the saddle blanket and packsaddle on. The horse stood motionless.

"You sure came up with a good idea there, Buck," said Neil.

The miner glowed with pride.

We lifted the packboxes to the saddle and hitched them on with the basket ropes.

"There is nothing to packing," said Neil. "I am going to ask Geddic for an assistant packer job when I see him next."

He placed his bedroll between the packboxes for the top pack.

"Nothing to do now but cinch her down."

He threw the canvas pack mantle over the load like a fisherman casting a net. The canvas made a swishing sound before dropping against the horse's flanks.

The filly threw up her head, startled. Then she reared, arched her back and kicked high. Neil and Buck sprang clear. I clung to the halter rope, trying to control the panicky animal. Being blindfolded, she followed the pull of the halter rope. The more I tried to control her, the more she came my way.

I backed into a patch of willows, fell over backward and stumbled about trying to regain my feet. Something hit me in the back of the head. I almost lost consciousness. The halter rope slipped from my hands.

I looked up into two concerned faces.

"I think you caught a hoof," said Neil. "How do you feel?"

I got to my knees. Something trickled down my neck.

In great alarm, I grabbed at the fluid, expecting to see my hand come away with blood. Instead, it came away with maple syrup.

"I'm all right," I said, relieved.

With a happy grin, Neil said, "It wasn't a hoof that hit you; it was a bottle of maple syrup. Too bad you got hit where you can't lick your wound."

The filly stood at the edge of the pasture, looking slatternly. The gunny sack hung from her halter, and ropes trailed from her packsaddle. She had bucked off her packboxes and their contents. The syrup bottle gave a few more convulsive gulps and then settled into a contented ooze. The pasture was strewn with tins, pots, frying pans and eating utensils.

"A true scene of disaster," I observed. "My brother would have appreciated this."

"I wonder if Bob Carey would," said Neil. "I remember now that he told us to use a gentle, experienced horse for a kitchen horse."

Neil and I walked over to the filly. She did not move. She had a long scratch on her nose; evidently she had run into a tree before the blindfold had come loose.

Neil reached out to grasp the halter shank. The animal backed away.

"Whoa, Scarface," Neil exclaimed. The horse had received her name.

As we led Scarface back to her dumped packboxes, Neil whispered, "If another brain rushes to Buck's head, ignore it."

"Don't be snide," I admonished. "It's not his fault we decorated the scenery with our groceries. It was the pack cover, not the blindfold, that scared the horse."

We tied Scarface to a tree and packed her without trouble. The solidity of the tree seemed to discourage her. To forestall any further catastrophes, we tied each of the other packhorses to the tree too.

After five hours of saddling, packing, making repairs and repacking, we headed out on the trail west. We had scarcely enough energy left to tip our hats farewell to the good-natured coal miner.

"Things always take longer when you have volunteer help," Neil remarked.

I took the lead, and the outfit trailed behind me into the Highwood Range, the first range of the Rocky Mountains. Dick, my mount, moved ahead with his usual enthusiasm. Behind us Neil played his harmonica. The ride began to fit into the dreams I had had of mountain trails. I marvelled at the broad sweep of forest in Junction Valley, and then the garland of cloud on the cliffs of Gibraltar Mountain.

The trail ended abruptly on a bank above Sheep Creek. A bridge had once carried the trail to the other side; apparently a flood had taken it away. I could see a path on the far side leading into the timber.

We made a short, steep detour to a ford upstream. I crossed easily on Dick. The filly I was leading followed willingly. Rex and Kit, experienced packhorses, saw the water only as a long drink. After they had tanked up, the four horses climbed another steep detour trail on the other side of the creek to regain the main trail.

I waited for Neil. The packhorses became impatient and wandered away to graze. I finally lost patience too and returned to the ford. Neil was in the middle of the river with a rope to his saddlehorn, skidding a reluctant Scarface into the water. The saddlehorse and packhorse changed positions in midstream. The filly came splashing out of the river in the lead, eager for dry land.

Neil rode up to me and stopped. "That proves the old saying: you can lead a horse to water but you have to pull it into the drink."

We rode under the cliffs of Gibraltar Mountain into a high valley. At the timberline at the base of Storm Mountain we came upon a collection of shacks called Burns Mine. An old freight wagon was parked beside a shack, marooned in the mountains now that the bridge below was gone.

An elderly man emerged from the shack. A large curved pipe complicated his German accent. "Welcome, welcome to Burns Mine. They leave me here like that wagon. We fall to the pieces together."

27

Bill Sommers was the watchman at the defunct coal mine. He had migrated from the Swiss Alps to the Canadian Rockies, only temporarily losing elevation. In fact he had risen a thousand feet or so. He was lonely; since autumn he had seen only Bob Carey who brought him grub from time to time. Neil and I were the first outfit on the Sheep Creek Trail in the 1932 season.

"You will stay, you will stay." It sounded like a plea.

"You bet," Neil exclaimed, swinging out of the saddle. "You have good grass here. We seen only rocks and trees all afternoon."

We unpacked the horses beside an abandoned shack. While I moved our gear inside, Neil took the horses to the grass.

We cooked supper in Bill Sommers' shack. He filled the room with stories of winter snowslides and spring floods, both of which had threatened to carry his shack into Sheep Creek. Billows of smoke erupted from his pipe at each dramatic pause.

With full bellies, a warm cabin, the sudden beat of rain on the roof and a hard-to-follow German Swiss accent, Neil and I disgraced ourselves. We fell asleep at the table while Bill was in full oratorical flight.

We awoke shivering. The cabin was dark. Bill Sommers snored on his bunk. We searched with our hands for our blankets and unrolled them onto the floor.

"What you gonna do? You gonna sleep all day?"

I opened an eye. "What time is it, Bill?"

"Eight-thirty."

Neil mumbled, "That's only half an hour of sleep; we fell asleep at eight."

"Twelve and a half," Bill corrected. He still took at face value everything Neil said.

Neil sat up. "Twelve and a half hours fighting this floor. No wonder I'm wore out."

Rain pelted the shake roof.

"I don't think we should travel today," said Neil. "We didn't bring gumboots for the horses. They might get their feet wet."

We cooked and ate hotcakes for an hour or so, soaking them

in "the hair of the dog that bit Cliff," as Neil called the maple syrup.

When the rain let up, Bill suggested that Neil and I take his rifle and try for a deer. We set out with the gun, skinning knives, field glasses and uncertainty about the legal hunting season.

"I have never seen a deer," I admitted to Neil. "What part of it do you shoot at?"

"The heart."

"Where exactly is the heart on a deer?"

Neil was silent for a moment. "Aim for the head," he said finally.

We soon climbed above the scattered trees of the valley and emerged onto high grassy slopes covered with flowers.

A shaft of sunlight broke through the clouds that raced above us. The drab, grey mountains burst into colour.

I was avid for more of this beauty. "Let's climb to the top of the pass!"

Mountain scenery did not inflame Neil the way it did me. He wanted to kill a deer. Besides, he objected to walking when we had horses for the job. "Horsemen don't walk."

We parted, Neil taking the rifle. I climbed to the top of the pass called Rickettes Gap. On the other side I looked down on a broad valley through which roared Misty Creek. Above it rose Misty Mountain, snow-covered and serrated. I stood and admired the scene until clouds swept down from the peaks to join others rising from the valley. I was enveloped in mist. Landmarks disappeared. In no time I was confused. There was only one thing to do: go downhill until I reached the trail.

I did better than just reach the trail; I struck the Burns Mine camp dead on. Neil was already there, listening to Bill and drinking coffee. I bragged about my pathfinding accuracy and soon forgot that it was largely luck.

After supper the cabin was silent. I was busy preserving my adventures in a notebook. Bill, having related the stories he had been so eager to tell, puffed on his pipe and ruminated. Neil reached into a pocket and pulled out his mouth organ. There followed a mournful version of *Home Sweet Home* and an even more lugubrious *Cowboy's Lament.*

I sensed that we had to move farther into the mountains the next day or Neil would be hitting the backtrail.

"Well, Kananaskis Lakes tomorrow," I said cheerily the moment the mouth organ stopped sobbing.

Neil responded, "Maybe we should head back to the prairies. I'm sick of this rain. Just think how miserable we would be in a tent."

"That is sissy talk," I chided. "Besides, on the prairies you complained because there was no rain."

Neil returned to the *Cowboy's Lament* and then put the mouth organ back into his pocket.

"Bill wants out of this place too. He figures maybe we could get him a job on a farm, feeding stock or something. This lonely mountain life is too tough on a guy, even a Swiss."

"There are no jobs on the prairies. You know that as well as I do. At least Bill has a job here."

"I told him that you just finished learning to be a teacher and maybe you could get him a job as a helper, watching the kids at recess or cleaning the classroom or something."

"The fact that I am going to become a teacher just proves how desperate the job situation is," I said.

Bill spoke up. "Well, boys, I am old man now. All my life leads to Burns Mine. I die soon. I go defunct in broken-down shack."

Tears rolled down the old man's cheeks. Neil and I had never seen an adult cry before—it had never occurred to us that they could. We were confounded.

Neil, as usual, tried to overcome embarrassment with words. He blurted out, "You are going to put out the fire in your pipe, Bill."

Somehow the gauche remark made us all grin. We went to bed before the sadness returned.

In the morning, before the sun had broken over Burns Mountain, Neil went out to gather the horses. I stayed with Bill to whip up some Coyote Brand Pancake Mix.

Trying to sound casual, I said, "Bill, I may be able to help you move out of Burns Mine next spring, depending on how my teaching job goes."

I wanted to give the old man hope that he would not be trapped at Burns Mine for the rest of his life. The despair that he had expressed the previous evening troubled me. It was at odds with what I had expected to find in the mountains; to me the mountains represented freedom and adventure.

As soon as I heard the thud of hooves outside, I began tossing batter on the griddle. Neil burst into the shack with a happy grin. The fine weather had brought back his good spirits.

The horses were frisky after their day of rest. The young ones skittered about but stood still when we set a blanket and saddle on them. They were beginning to take their job seriously. They were educated.

Bill Sommers bade us goodbye. "You welcome at my shack when you coming back. You welcome like flowers in the springtime."

Beyond Burns Mine the trail disappeared into washouts. We crossed Sheep Creek time and again, seeking a trail that had disappeared with the stream bank on which it had been traced.

Eventually the country levelled out. We passed Elbow Lake and struggled through bogs at the headwaters of Elbow Creek.

As we started down the declivity toward Kananaskis Lakes, Scarface tried to edge Kit out of the favoured position behind the lead horse. Kit nearly forced the young social climber off the trail. Chastened, the filly fell into line ahead of Rex; in spite of his royal moniker, he did not care whose tail he followed.

At Kananaskis Lakes we halted in front of the ranger's cabin. The ranger stepped outside. We told him where we had come from and where we intended to go and asked about grass for the horses.

"Go down the Elk Lakes Trail to the woman," said the ranger. "But keep your horses out of the fenced pasture."

"Thanks," I said. I wanted to talk more, but the man's demeanour did not invite conversation.

As we rode away, Neil repeated, puzzled, "Go down to the

31

The Lady
of Lower
Kananaskis Lake.

woman?"

I took the lead again. In a few minutes I came to a life-sized carving in a pine tree.

I hollered back to Neil. "I've met the woman."

"What are you talking about? I don't see anyone."

He rode past the packhorses to where I was.

"She's beautiful," he said.

Neil led his horse to the pole gate of the nearby pasture. "What do you say we do our eating in the pasture and let the horses do theirs outside? The levellest ground for the tent is inside the fence."

He slid the poles back on the gate. I herded the packhorses through. After we had unsaddled them we moved them back outside the fence and reset the poles.

In the middle of the night I awoke to the sound of animals grazing near our tent.

"Neil!"

"What?" It was apparent from his voice that he had been awake and listening to the sound too.

"What are we going to do about the horses?"

"You can do what you like. I am not chasing horses in the dark. Maybe they aren't even ours."

A few hours later, just after dawn, the ranger put his head between the flaps of our tent door. "What the hell do you boys think you are doing?"

"We aren't doing nothing but sleeping," mumbled Neil.

"Your horses are in my pasture. I told you to keep them out."

"They rubbed down the bars of the gate," Neil replied hopefully.

This infuriated the ranger. "I have news for you—the bars are still up. I will have you squirts run out of here like a couple of turpentined cats if you don't remove your horses from my grass."

We pulled on our clothes and stumbled outside. The ranger was dropping the poles on the gate. Neil and I trudged through the dew-wet grass and chased our horses out. Then we insisted that the ranger accompany us on an inspection of the fence. He came along reluctantly, grumbling.

We traced the fence line over a low ridge. On the far side a section of fence lay on the ground.

"You see," said Neil triumphantly. "You came at us as snarly as a cave full of bears, and all the time it's your own fence that's fallen on its face."

Evidently the ranger had not bothered to check the fence since his return to the Kananaskis Lakes station after his winter in town.

Neil and I returned to our tent feeling virtuous. It put Neil into an ambitious frame of mind. "Now that we are up so early, let's go to Elk Lakes."

I was astonished at the proposal; Neil's usual suggestion was to hit the backtrail. Crossing the Front Ranges of the Rocky Mountains

Kananaskis Lake.

had given him spirit. And me too. It was as though a cord attaching us to the prairies had been broken. We had new confidence in our ability to challenge the mountains.

We rode south beyond the meadows and up into the timber. Dick moved ahead enthusiastically, as interested in new country as Neil and I were. He was a conscientious horse. Without the responsibility of the pack animals behind him, his mood seemed lighter.

We crossed the level meadows of the pass and then started downhill along a creek that ran south. I slowed Dick until Neil and Jimmy came abreast of us. I pointed at the south-flowing creek and remarked wonderingly, "That water flows into the Pacific Ocean."

Neil looked down at it intently. "It looks the same as the water we've been seeing all along."

"It's not what it looks like, it's where it's going that makes it special."

"Just like us."

We rode through the trees to Elk Lake, a pretty piece of water tucked into an amphitheatre of mountains and glaciers. We sat on

34

our horses and gazed at the view. The horses swept their tails from side to side and shook their manes against the mosquitoes. The scene was magnificent. But now that we had seen it, there was nothing more to do.

"Nice," said Neil, nodding his head in affirmation. Then we reined our mounts about and returned to Kananaskis Lakes.

As we neared our camping place we came upon a band of twenty-eight horses. "We have company," I said.

"There is absolutely no doubt about it. I bet it's old Geddic," said Neil. He added thoughtfully, "Tomorrow we are going to have to pack up with him watching us."

Kananaskis Lake was lined with tents. There were two campfires. The desperation with which the people who surrounded them fought mosquitoes showed them to be dudes.

Neil and I unsaddled our horses beside our gear. I suggested, "After we eat, let's go over and get acquainted."

"You bet," said Neil. "You talk to old Geddic about trails while I meet the women. It looks like there are all kinds of them from running to draft types."

After supper we rummaged through the packboxes for a mirror. I was rather proud of the reflection I saw. After only four days I had a good start on a full beard.

Neil broke into my contemplation. "Looks like the east end of a horse going west, doesn't it?"

"Well, well, here are the lads who are going to teach me how to pack horses," remarked Geddic as we approached his campfire.

"And you are going to teach us how to tell stories," replied Neil. "You go first."

"Pull up a stump and sit in, then. There's the cups and there's the pot. Lap your lips over my cook's good java."

There were ten dudes in Geddic's party, mostly women, only two of them young enough to be bait for Neil's and my glances. They seemed rightly fascinated by our western appearance. We had donned our chaps and stetsons in order to enhance the effect, even though wearing chaps while afoot was cumbersome.

We were briefly grateful to Geddic when he told the admiring group, "These boys put on the best horse pack I ever seen."

Neil said humbly, "Thanks for the compliment."

Geddic replied with a grin, "You are most welcome. It's the first of them stories you was asking for."

Mosquitoes rose from the moist ground along the lake. They were not deterred by the smoke from the fires, although the dudes were. Conversation degenerated into complaints about smoke and mosquitoes. The dudes drifted away to their tents. They had nothing to say to farm boys dressed in cowboy clothes. They were seeking something else.

Before dawn Neil went for our horses while I cooked breakfast. It was too cold for mosquitoes and too early for Geddic. We hoped to get away before either roused.

By the time we were stowing our cooking gear, Geddic's cook and choreman were building a fire and carrying water from the lake. The wrangler and Geddic came out of their tents and walked to the fire. Geddic looked our way and bellowed, "Morning, boys. Looks like you got up before breakfast today." The blast would have awakened his trail riders, and was probably meant to.

We packed Rex and Kit first. Then we tackled the young horses. We did not expect trouble with the gentle one, the one we had named Crouch from the way she walked under leaning trees. Neil was on the left side of Crouch and I was on the right, each of us holding a packbox and ready to lift it to the basket rope on the saddle.

Neil said, "Okay."

We lifted in unison. Neil hitched his box down. I didn't catch the rope quite right. The box began to slip from my hands, and I lifted a knee to support it. I was a little too close to the packhorse; my knee caught her in the belly.

The startled horse bucked. My packbox continued its descent. Neil's packbox flew out of its hitch and hit the ground with a crash, emptying its contents at the horse's feet.

Crouch took off at a trot toward the ranger's cabin. Neil ran

Neil Mackay fording the Kananaskis River.

after her hollering, "Whoa, whoa," and words less kind.

Geddic strolled over to observe at close hand our humiliation. He was grinning. "Looks like your horse does not want to be decorated today," he drawled. "I will help you pack when your partner gets back with the horse. You seem to want to get away right early."

He inspected the packs on Rex and Kit but made no comment. I reloaded the spilled gear into Crouch's packboxes.

Neil returned with the horse in a few minutes, holding the halter rope in one hand and a loaf of bread in the other. He explained, "The ranger stopped the horse at his cabin. He said he had baked bread last night and he thought we might like some."

Geddic instructed us as we packed the two fillies. He did not teach us anything basic that we did not know already but he showed us many fine points that would make our packing easier and faster.

We rode south along Lower Kananaskis Lake and swung around the end of it to the crossing place between the two lakes.

The ford was slow but deep. Dick, our tallest horse, crossed easily. Rex and Kit, the experienced packhorses, followed. I tied Rex to a tree on the far side, believing that Kit would stay with him. But the packhorse followed Dick and me back across the river, perhaps hoping that we were returning home at last. My reason for recrossing was to help Neil bring the young horses over. They were smaller and lighter than the older horses and were in danger of losing their footing.

Neil tied a rope to Crouch's halter and handed it to me. I wrapped a couple of turns around my saddlehorn and started back across the river. Crouch followed willingly. Kit crossed again right behind us.

Neil tied a rope to Scarface's halter and set out into the river on Jimmy. He expected to pay out rope as he crossed. But Scarface was not to be left alone. She plunged in and followed closely in Jimmy's wake.

We rode along the north shore of Upper Kananaskis Lake and across a meadow. The mountains closed in. Sheer cliffs made of sedimentary layers set on end rose on either side. We were in the very heart of the Rocky Mountains.

We followed the Kananaskis River north on a steep trail which wound through a thicket of short spruce trees. Snow slides had mowed the forest to a height of seven feet above the ground.

Just as I was about to break onto open alpine country, I looked back at Neil and the packhorses. Neil had turned Jimmy around and was riding back down the trail. I was puzzled but waited patiently. In a few minutes Neil returned and signalled me to go on.

We crossed a low ridge above Lawson Lake and entered a large basin. At this place the vegetation had scarcely greened up. There was no grass, just alpine plants, some growing at the very edge of banks of melting snow. We could take our hungry horses no farther.

We unpacked at an old fire circle and let the horses go free. "There is so little feed here, we should let them graze unfettered until dark," I said.

"We can let them graze free all night," replied Neil confidently.

"Are you crazy? They will drift back to Kananaskis Lakes and maybe all the way home."

"It's all looked after," said Neil smugly.

"Then you can go after them tomorrow on your own."

"Okay."

I was perplexed by Neil's attitude.

"Stop being so inscrutable," I demanded.

"If you are going to use words that run four to the pound, I will have to tell you in simple words why we do not need to hobble or picket the horses tonight. It is because I put a bar across the trail in that tight patch of spruce trees on the way up."

"You are smarter than you look."

"Then I must be a genius."

At dawn I went to the creek for water, noting that our horses were still on the meadow. The creek bed was almost dry; the cold night had halted the snow melt that fed it. When I returned to camp Neil was up, trying to start the fire with frosty twigs. "This is the coldest I have ever been on July 8," he said.

The summit of North Kananaskis Pass was little more than a mile from our camp and not much higher. We rode through scattered larches to Maude Lake, a green tarn with snowbanks soaking their feet at the shore. Our horses picked their way through the shallow water and then climbed onto the snowdrifts covering the east side of the pass. The snow was so hard that it scarcely recorded our passage.

On the top of the pass, straddling the Alberta–British Columbia border, we stopped to admire the view. The horses' tails sailed in the westerly wind. We had to hold down our hats. Below us was a deep valley. Beyond, as far as we could see, were mountains.

We dismounted and checked cinches and loads on the packhorses. It was a long, steep way down to our next camp beside the Palliser River.

The trail left the snow in the pass and wound down through broken rock and boulders, and eventually into timber. The horses seemed eager to leave the high country. Sometimes they slid on their haunches over patches of loose rock; they kept up a steady, determined pace, not balking even at fallen trees but struggling over or around them with a will.

Within two hours we stepped onto a gravel bar on the Palliser River. The air was warm and soft. For all the sense of freedom the alpine country had given us, it had also made us feel uneasy. I sensed that it tolerated only briefly creatures that stood tall like men and horses. Even trees had hugged the ground there.

Neil Mackay at Maude Lake on the summit of North Kananaskis Pass.

The upper Palliser River was clear and shallow. It wandered wilfully back and forth across its wide bed. We travelled directly down it, fording its shallow channels again and again.

When the gradient steepened, the river got itself together, and we had to leave it. There were trails leading in every direction. The country obviously abounded in large animals. Time and again their trails led us astray, beginning boldly at the river's edge, going a few hundred yards, then evaporating like mist. After each trail's disappearance, we had to fight through fallen timber, tiring the horses.

Eventually we discovered a blazed trail and stuck with it, ignoring the alluring paths that sprouted everywhere. Late in the afternoon we came to a meadow and an old corral. We stopped and set up camp.

In the morning Neil put his saddle on Crouch. He wanted to know if the filly would make a satisfactory saddlehorse. She seemed to have a good set of brains. She had learned to swing her pack past trees without many collisions. This was desirable behaviour in a saddlehorse; it saved a rider's legs.

I set out ahead on Dick and turned to watch Neil mount. Crouch did not buck or even crowhop, even when Neil poked her in the ribs with his boot heel. They trotted around the meadow, then joined the end of the packstring.

At the top of a hill I looked back to see how the packs were riding. Jimmy and Rex were right behind me, and in a few moments Scarface and Kit rounded the corner in the trail. We waited. The horses swished their tails.

Where were Neil and Crouch?

I dismounted. "Take care of the packhorses for a few minutes, Dick," I said to my horse. I walked back down the trail.

Through the trees came the words, "You boneheaded piece of crowbait!"

Neil was standing in a small creek tugging on a halter rope. Crouch was tugging back. The horse had a seven-hundred pound advantage.

41

"What is the matter, Neil?" I said. "Is your new saddlehorse more than you can handle? You look madder than a squeezed hornet."

Neil let the halter rope go slack and turned to look at me. There were tears in his eyes. "We crossed Sheep Creek, we crossed Pocaterra Creek, we crossed the Kananaskis River, we waded down the Palliser River, and this senseless animal will not step across this trickle."

He threw the end of the halter rope down in disgust. It splashed. The horse backed up a few steps.

I stepped across the creek on some rocks below the ford. Neil waded toward me and picked up the halter rope again. Once again the filly went to the water's edge and then balked. I slapped her on the rump with my hand to no effect. I tried a switch. Still no result.

Neil and I changed positions. My boots had hardly filled with water before Neil landed a whack on the filly's rump that sent her across the stream in a rush. I was nearly bowled over.

As we wrung our socks, I asked, "Do you think you have a promising saddlehorse there?"

"A few minutes ago I could have ground her up for bird bait. I will give her one more chance. Tonight I will mark her report card. If she fails, she stays a packhorse."

"That's what she probably would prefer," I said. "You and your saddle weigh a hundred pounds more than her pack. And she can pick grass along the trail when she runs free. With you on her back she has to work harder and eat less. You said you thought she might have brains."

I reined Dick onto a deeply indented trail that swung away from the Palliser River. The lack of blazes perturbed me but the width and depth of the path convinced me that it was the correct one. It led to a pond whose edges had been trampled by the hooves of hundreds of animals.

Neil looked at me in disgust. "I did not expect to reach the Pacific Ocean so soon," he said.

"A mineral lick," I explained defensively. "I thought you and the horses might like to see it."

Neil wheeled Crouch around. In the lead he could not hold to the horse trail any better than I had. He led us into an old burn full of snags and windfalls. The wind blowing up the valley rattled loose bark and set leaning snags to groaning against each other like anguished souls.

Neil dismounted and took the axe from the top of Kit's pack. He flailed away at the hard, dry wood. He seemed driven by some fierce emotion. When sweat was dripping from his nose, I offered to take a spell with the axe. He set the axe down surprisingly gently and said, "You have to go at this like you was killing snakes or you don't get nowheres." He would not admit it, but his hard work with the axe was atonement for leading us into the labyrinth.

We gradually worked our way out of the burn and back to the river. Green timber on the far bank promised easier going. The ford was swift but shallow. All the horses followed Dick's sensible route across, except for Scarface. With perverse determination, the filly headed toward the lower end of the shallow. She stepped suddenly from the edge of the gravel into a pool. The current caught her, drove her against a boulder and then swung her around and capsized her. She reached shallow water, struggled to her feet and completed the ford, emerging from the river with water pouring from her pack.

"Whose blankets are in the top pack?" asked Neil.

"Yours, I think."

Neil directed familiar words of abuse at the filly.

She stood quietly dripping, somewhat wiser; better educated.

I scouted ahead on Dick while Neil held the rest of the outfit at the crossing place. A faint trail enticed me. It climbed above the river and crept along the brink of a cutbank.

Dick became restive and finally refused to go on. Apparently he was aware of some danger I could not perceive.

My nose discovered the cause of Dick's alarm before my eyes did. The foul odour of rotting flesh rose from a mound just ahead of us. The remains of a deer, partly covered with dirt and branches, lay in our path.

I reined Dick about. He wanted to retreat as much as I did, but

43

the ledge was too narrow to turn on. A hind leg went over the edge of the trail onto the loose gravel of the cutbank. I wished I had dismounted, but it was too late to be wise now. I leaned forward and cried, "Come on, Dick." He scrambled wildly for a moment, then heaved up onto the ledge.

I stepped out of the saddle on the uphill side. Both I and my horse were shaking. I moved ahead carefully and pulled the reins over his head. We looked down onto the boulders that had awaited us at the bottom of the hill. Then we walked briskly back the way we had come.

"Well?" said Neil.

"Well, you just about had to finish this trip on your own," I replied. I described the remains of the deer I had come across and how close I had come to tumbling with my horse into the Palliser River.

"What do you think killed the deer?" asked Neil.

"Probably a cougar. Maybe a grizzly."

"Let's clear out of here."

Neil crossed the Palliser again to look for a trail on the north side. Presently I saw him high on a cutbank. He motioned me to come.

Snubbing Scarface tightly to my saddlehorn to forestall a repeat of her aquatic acrobatics, I nudged Dick into the river. The other horses followed.

As we drew up before him, Neil exclaimed, "This is the place where we switch our packs from horses to mountain goats."

The trail that Neil had found ended at a long clay cutbank. The Palliser River roared over a bed of boulders a hundred feet below. The cutbank extended hundreds of feet above.

"It is not as bad as it looks," declared Neil.

"I can see everything there is to see—and it looks bad to me," I retorted.

"Let me present you with good news," said Neil. He reached behind a tree and produced a shovel and a pick.

I grinned with relief. "So we aren't the first pilgrims to face this

Neil Mackay devouring a stack of flapjacks.

problem."

"Which do you want? You have second choice. I'm taking the shovel."

We hacked and dug at the clay for half an hour, improving on the blisters we had received from the axe handle in the burn. At the far side of the cutbank we found another shovel and pick for the use of travellers coming from the other direction.

We moved into the shade of the forest to unsweat. When we returned to the cutbank our trail seemed to have disappeared. The disturbed clay had dried to the same colour as the rest of the cutbank.

"We know it is there," said Neil. "All we have to do is convince the horses."

We returned the pick and shovel to the place where Neil had found them. Then I led Dick onto the nick we had made in the cutbank. I was grateful that he followed readily, for I would not have coerced him. I respected his judgement as much as my own. Neil encouraged the packhorses to follow, and they did, confidently. The horses seemed braver than we were, perhaps because at each step they still had three feet on the ground; Neil and I had only one.

Not far from the cutbank we had to ford the Albert River which comes into the Palliser from the north. We climbed out of it to get past a canyon and then made a long descent to a flat on Little Elk Creek.

Little Elk Creek valley offered splendid pasture for our horses and magnificent red-barked ponderosa pines under which to set our tent. While I gathered firewood, Neil emptied the packboxes that Scarface had immersed in the Palliser River. He spread his wet blankets over a couple of small pine trees to dry.

Neil had the same dour look that he had had at Burns Mine just before he suggested returning to the prairies. I made a few light remarks to divert his thoughts. "They will dry fast in this warm breeze," I said, referring to his blankets.

"They won't be dry before the storm hits."

"What storm?"

"The warm air means a storm is coming."

"No, it means we are out of the high country."

We started to argue, our tempers worn thin by the heat and hard travel. The topic under dispute scarcely mattered and soon drifted away from a discussion of warm air. Neil recited our narrow escapes from death, even elaborating on my encounter with the dead deer, which he had not seen. He concluded by stating that our expedition was as much fun as washing greasy frying pans in a cold creek.

I let him have the last word. Neither he nor the horses would be inclined to backtrail now. We were too far from home. Only a short climb over the gentle Kootenay Range would complete our journey through the Rocky Mountains, and I was beginning to feel pride in the bunch of us.

Next morning we rode through rolling hills. Topping a little rise, we looked down on the Kootenay River sweeping out of the north.

Because I rode the tallest and wisest horse, there was no doubt that I should attempt the crossing first. I chose a place just above a riffle where the water was slick.

Dick stepped off the gravel bar and splashed into the shallows. The water was soon stirrup deep and rose up the saddle. Dick seemed to lean against the current; I was afraid that he was going to lose his footing. I had only the toes of my boots in the stirrups, ready to come loose from the saddle.

I talked to my horse, told him to take it easy, told him he was doing fine. He concentrated on his job and moved ahead steadily. The Kootenay River was only a few hundred feet across, but I felt as though I was spending a big part of my life in it.

Finally the saddle emerged from the water. Dick moved ahead quicker, his shoulder muscles surging as he made for dry land.

The ford was too deep for the packhorses to wade without soaking our gear. I motioned to Neil not to cross there. He set off downstream, driving the packhorses ahead of him.

I turned downstream, too, and soon came to a good trail which led to a broad, shallow ford. I dismounted and sat on the bank. While I waited for Neil to appear on the opposite bank, I wrung my socks.

I became puzzled by Neil's tardiness. It was apparent that he had missed the crossing place. I had to track him down. I crossed the river in swift, shallow water not even to the stirrups.

The trail from the ford soon intercepted another one that parallelled the river. There were lots of horse tracks to show that Neil had missed the turnoff.

I nudged Dick into a fast walk. When we emerged from the forest onto a river bar, we were greeted by a shout from the opposite shore. Neil sat on Jimmy, surrounded by four dripping packhorses.

47

He had swum the river in a gentle stretch of deep water.

"Go upstream and I'll meet you," I hollered and then turned around.

I was furious. Neil had missed the easy ford and soaked the entire outfit in a deep one. I was so busy gathering words for our reunion that I missed the trail to the ford myself. I let my carefully gathered words scatter.

I turned back to the ford and crossed the river. The packhorses emerged from the forest ahead of Neil's insults. He was in a bad temper again.

I resolved to be kindly to him. "You did a good job of getting the horses across the river," I said. "Nothing can stop us now. We are safe and sound on the west side of the Kootenay River. We will reach the Columbia Valley tomorrow—and then on to the Purcells. Let's unpack and dry our gear."

Before he could reflect on the word Purcells, I asked him to help me get the pack off Crouch so that I could get at my blankets and hang them out to dry.

"They should dry fast in this warm breeze," I said cheerily.

"There is going to be a storm tonight," asserted Neil.

"Mmmm," I replied.

Our climb over the Kootenay Range, the last of the Rocky Mountains, was steep and tedious but took only a day. The trail wound through timber the whole distance. Neil entertained himself by composing invective for the packhorses, particularly Scarface. It was obvious he loved the filly.

In the afternoon we descended along Windermere Creek, watching it grow from a brook to a goodly stream. As we lost elevation the trees grew farther apart and undergrowth disappeared. Late in the day we rode out onto a shoulder of a ridge and looked into the Columbia Valley, broad and blue in the haze. At the bottom lay Windermere Lake surrounded by bright green fields.

"We have done it. We have crossed the Rockies," I said with satisfaction.

"What are those things on the other side of the valley?"

"What things?"

"Those big things with trees on the bottom and snow on top."

"Those are the Purcell Mountains."

"They look just like the mountains we just came through."

I had to agree. Our triumph seemed arbitrary. Mountain ranges extended all the way from the prairies to the Pacific Ocean. I wondered how long it would take to go all the way by horseback.

In the Columbia Valley two young riders came up behind us and slowed down to talk horses. We clomped across the plank bridge spanning the Columbia River. At the edge of Athalmer we stopped at a shack, and our two acquaintances introduced us to Fredrickson. He told us to throw our gear in his stable for the night and sleep there, too, if we wished. "Just let your horses run in the village," he said.

The sun was setting behind the Purcells, throwing half the valley into shadow. We unpacked in a rush and put a bell on Kit. Then we turned the horses loose to feed in town and set out to do the same ourselves.

"I can hardly wait for a café meal," said Neil. "Your cooking has shrunk my equator."

"You did half the cooking yourself," I pointed out.

"That's why I am only half-starved."

The waitress was a sprightly teenager with freckles. She seemed impressed by our black cowboy hats, untidy appearance and smell. "You smell something like a forest fire," she said.

Our expectations concerning a café meal were severely damaged when the girl said, "After seven o'clock we don't serve meals. But if you want bacon and eggs, mom will cook you some— mom's the cook."

"Suits me fine," said Neil gallantly. "I haven't eaten unburnt bacon and eggs since I left Alberta."

While we ate, the girl stood at our table to listen to Neil tell stories about our trip. He embellished our adventures shamelessly.

"Oh, I would like to take a trip like that!" exclaimed the girl.

"We have an extra horse," lied Neil.

With evident regret the girl said, "Mom would never let me."

As we left, I said to Neil, "Geddic would be proud of you."

Neil grinned. "I liked her freckles. She looks like she swallowed a dollar and broke out in pennies."

Back at Fredrickson's place mosquitoes rose from the wet bottomland. They kept us awake most of the night. We could hear Kit's bell clanging in town. Perhaps the citizens of Athalmer were being kept awake too.

"I think we should get up early," said Neil. "I'll sneak across town and get the bunch before they are arrested for disturbing the peace."

After rounding up our horses, we wrote exultant letters home. We had crossed the Rockies and we were proud of it. We took the letters to the Athalmer post office and returned with groceries in our arms. We had left the horses—and our big black hats—behind at Fredrickson's because we did not want to be recognized as the owners of the horse bell.

We rode northwest through Athalmer and then Wilmer, past irrigated farms and orchards and finally into the narrow valley of Horsethief Creek. We stopped at a cabin in a grassy clearing. The cabin promised a haven from mosquitoes. We were very sleepy.

Neil hobbled the horses while I got the stove hot for supper. The warmth of the cabin made us so drowsy we were asleep before the alpenglow had left the peaks.

The next day we rode up the valley of Horsethief Creek through forest and beneath rock faces tinselled with streams. We stopped to camp at the foot of glacier-topped mountains.

After our campfire had been burning for awhile I said to Neil, "The smoke isn't chasing us around the fire the way it usually does. I wonder why it drifts steadily downhill."

"Because that is the way the breeze is blowing," replied Neil indulgently.

The breeze was barely perceptible yet it seeped into my blankets all night. No amount of turning and tucking prevented my uphill side from becoming chilled.

At dawn I got up and built a brisk campfire. I ruminated about the drift of cold air that I could scarcely feel though it had chilled me to the bone.

When the sun finally lifted over the trees, I went into the tent to wake Neil. My blankets were wrapped around him. I let him sleep.

"Hey, you sound like you are sawing wood and hitting lots of knots," Neil shouted. Under the warm sun, I had fallen asleep.

While I whipped up some Coyote Brand Pancake Mix that we had bought at Athalmer, Neil moved the horses' pickets. The animals were to have a holiday. We were so sure that the Lake of the Hanging Glacier was just over the ridge that we were going on foot.

We climbed to the top of the ridge and were disappointed. There was no lake. But we glimpsed a glacier ahead and headed for it.

Forest gave way to alpine tundra, and tundra gave way to glacial rubble. A silt-loaded stream emerged from the snout of the glacier, and cold air emanated from the ice cave that the stream had carved.

"Do you feel that cold air?" I asked Neil.

"Of course."

"Now we know where the cold breeze came from last night. We have had another mountain lesson: do not sleep below a glacier."

"I won't be using that lesson much," said Neil.

The glacier extended to the rock wall of the mountain. There was no lake.

We returned to camp and gathered in the horses. I wanted to search for the Lake of the Hanging Glacier on our way back to the Columbia Valley.

Neil refused. "You have seen pictures of it. Why look for scenery you can see in a magazine?"

"A picture is just a representation. I want to see the real thing."

"I figure a picture is scenery without mosquitoes."

"We learned more about glaciers today than an encyclopedia full of pictures could have shown us. Pictures are not experience," I exclaimed. "They are the residue of experience."

Neil frowned. "I would keep arguing if I knew what you are

talking about."

He returned to the job at hand, packing Kit. "Help me pull this diamond tight—and don't give slack this time."

"I never give slack," I retorted. "I know how to pack a horse as well as you do."

Neil grinned. He knew I was touchy because I could not find the Lake of the Hanging Glacier on a trail built for dudes.

We dropped down the trail with the horses toward some grass we had seen on the way up. It was farther than we remembered. Dusk crept out of the forest. Suddenly a man appeared in front of me with his arms outstretched.

"Hello," I blurted.

"Hello. You are travelling late. I heard horses and thought they was mine pulling out."

"We didn't see any horses."

"I put 'em across the creek in a patch of good grass. I figured it would hold 'em. Just to be sure I will block the way with a few poles after you boys ride by."

Around the next bend in the trail we reached the grass we had remembered. At the edge of it stood three tents, a heap of saddles and gear, and a campfire nearly out.

The man returned and threw some wood on his fire. Then he walked over to where Neil and I were struggling in the fading light to hobble our horses.

"Looks like everyone else in my outfit hit the sack the moment I left. Have you et?"

"No."

"Come over to my fire with your grub then. There is no point in building another fire."

We dug out a pot, canned beans and a couple of spoons from the kitchen box and went over to get acquainted. The guide was Nixon from Windermere. He had eight horses, a wrangler and a cook.

"That is a good-sized crew," I observed. "We met a large party like yours at Kananaskis Lakes a couple weeks ago."

"Kananaskis Lakes!" exclaimed Nixon. "You boys have done some travelling."

Neil and I were pleased to have impressed a professional guide. We told him about our journey across the Rocky Mountains. Then the conversation turned to the Lake of the Hanging Glacier—we had to admit that we could not find it.

Nixon explained, "Just up the trail a ways there is a big blaze on a tree on the other side of the creek. That is where you turn off."

"I'm going tomorrow," I declared.

Neil made no objection. Instead he turned to Nixon and asked, "Are there any women in your outfit?"

"Just one. The best client I ever had. She is always happy about everything and interested in everything. She is from the eastern States and has lots of money. I don't know why she wants to rough it in the bush—but I am glad she does."

Neil turned to me. "Cliff, I have already told you I'm not interested in the Lake of the Hanging Glacier. I'll stay here and look after the horses while you are away. They should be moved quite often while they are on this poor grass."

Next morning I saddled Dick, and before anyone else stirred, headed up the trail with blankets and a little food tied behind the cantle. The turnoff to the Lake of the Hanging Glacier was easy to find now that I knew what to look for.

At the blazed tree I turned Dick across Horsethief Creek. He climbed with a will. He was a kindred spirit when it came to exploring new country. We rose through a thick forest of spruce into scattered larch and pine. Before long the trees gave out onto a field of boulders.

I tied Dick to a larch tree and proceeded on foot. Marmots whistled and scampered for cover. I topped a ridge, and before me appeared a lake full of icebergs.

At the far side a glacier came down off a black mountain and terminated in a wall of dirty ice. A slab of ice toppled from the glacier wall, sending a wave across the lake and adding more icebergs.

I was reluctant to leave the Lake of the Hanging Glacier; I had

The Lake of the Hanging Glacier in the Purcell Mountains.

put a lot of effort into getting to it. Yet there was nothing to do once I had looked at the scene—and that did not take long. I took a photograph, my trophy of a successful hunt.

I returned to Dick and descended to the ford on Horsethief Creek. Nixon's outfit had set up camp at the ford. I met the young man who was cook, the boy who was horse wrangler and an elderly woman who was the client. The woman was full of energy and enthusiasm. She exclaimed about my solo trip to the Lake of the Hanging Glacier, as excited about others' adventures as her own.

In the morning I added Coyote Brand Pancake Mix to Nixon's

batter and joined his bunch for breakfast. "Pad out your belly good," advised the outfitter. "Your partner has likely eaten all your grub. There is nothing to whet a man's appetite like sitting around camp doing nothing."

The boy wrangler on Nixon's crew brought in three of their horses. Nixon put a couple of leftover hotcakes on his horse's back and threw on his saddle. "Those were pretty leathery hotcakes, Bill," he teased the cook. "I hate to see 'em go to waste. If I use 'em on my saddlehorse today I will save a day's wear on my saddle blanket." The prank was meant as entertainment for the old lady.

Nixon, the boy and the woman set out for the Lake of the Hanging Glacier. I turned down the trail in the opposite direction on Dick.

I was met by a bogus Chinese laundryman at Neil's camp. "You like me wash you shirt?" he enquired, putting his hands together and bowing. The trees surrounding the camp were draped with drying clothes.

"I like you hit the trail," I replied. "Take in your washing, John Chinaman, and dismantle your rag house. We are packing up."

We rode into Wilmer in the Columbia Valley. Neil stopped at the general store to buy provisions. I went to the government office for a map of the Vermilion Range, the part of the Rocky Mountains we intended to tackle next.

The government agent was a gracious, grey-haired man. He discerned quickly that I loved maps; he brought out every one that he had of his district. We enjoyed an hour tracing my past and future trails, exploring valleys and mountain passes on a paper landscape.

Finally I said, "I need only the map of the Vermilion Range."

The government agent shook his head regretfully. "I'm sorry, I can't let you have it. It is the only copy I have."

I stood gazing at the coveted piece of paper, struggling briefly in a vain attempt to memorize the intricate lines that represented rivers and mountains. Then I had an idea.

I said to the agent, "Do you have pieces of blank white paper?"

"Yes, of course."

55

"If you will allow me, I can trace the map if I put it up against the window."

The man was dubious but he took some pieces of writing paper from his desk. I struggled with the large map and the small sheets of paper, trying to keep them lined up. No sooner was the arrangement co-ordinated than it would fall to the floor. To make matters worse, my hands began to sweat from the hot sun on the window. The moisture warped the paper so that it would not lie flat, which made tracing more difficult.

Finally the man said, "This is not going to work. I will give you the map."

"Oh, thank you!" I exclaimed. "I shall mail it back to you as soon as I get home." It was a heartfelt promise, but considering the conditions of packhorse travel, not a realistic one.

Neil was on the steps of the general store conversing with an attractive young woman. As I approached she entered the store.

"I got the map," I reported. "It looked like you were receiving instructions too."

"I asked her how to get to the bridge across the Columbia River."

"But you already knew that. We rode across it a few days ago."

Neil shrugged. "I wanted somebody new to talk to."

The ride along the road to Radium Hotsprings was slow and hot. Cars threw up billows of dust. Our horses moved at a speed that seemed a small improvement over a dead stop.

At length we arrived at Sinclair Gap, the western entrance to Kootenay National Park and the Rocky Mountains. The Gap was a narrow canyon a hundred feet or so deep and overhung by rock walls that nearly shut out the sky. It was scarcely wide enough for the road that ran through it.

There was a toll gate at the entrance to the canyon. I rode up to the booth and asked the attendant the price of admission for a horse. Tourists who had been photographing the canyon turned their cameras on us. The attendant, looking damp and wilted in his little kiosk, declared that he charged admission only for motor vehicles; pedestrians entered free, and the horses looked like pedestrians to him. "Just get through fast!"

Sinclair Canyon led us from the wide valley of the Columbia River into the close-together walls of Sinclair Creek. For three miles the road ran under great red cliffs.

We stopped at the first grass we saw. It surrounded an auto

Sinclair Canyon in Kootenay National Park.

camp near a small lake. The owner welcomed us; our horses would clip his grass and provide diversion for his guests. "Look, Mommy, the cowboys are going to sleep outside all night!"

We did not hobble or picket our horses. It seemed evident to us that no horse with any sense would leave good grass at the auto court for the slim pickings we had passed along the road.

In the morning our horses were gone. Neil picked up their tracks heading west toward Sinclair Canyon. He started out at a brisk walk with Jimmy's bridle in hand and returned an hour later with the bunch at a trot.

We were on the road at eight o'clock, an early start for us. Kootenay Valley proved to be as hot and tedious as the Columbia Valley. Neil brought out his harmonica and played his two tunes. The sound of the instrument ceased whenever an automobile approached. The vehicle would hammer past on the washboard, "Thump, thump, thump." Clouds of dust would roll over us. The dust would abate. The mouth organ would resume its lamentations.

Eventually I had had enough of the *Cowboy's Lament*. I wheeled Dick around and went back to talk to Neil.

"Don't you know any other tunes?"

"I know *Home Sweet Home*."

"I am aware of that. How about something else?"

"Well, teach me some. Sing a few bars."

I tried *Annie Laurie*. It sounded weak, but I believed I had the thing right.

Neil said, "You forgot to pack something when we left on this trip."

"What?"

"A jug to carry tunes in."

I returned to the head of the packstring. The mournful wail resumed at the other end.

At Kootenay Crossing we had the choice of taking the trail along the west bank of the Kootenay River or staying on the road which led easily through Vermilion Pass to Banff and the prairies. I expected Neil to suggest that we stay with the road. He was silent except for a sharp word to the packhorses. I turned onto the trail.

A few minutes later there was a great commotion behind me. I looked back. Packhorses were bucking through the forest, hitting trees with their packs. Neil was reining Jimmy about and heading back down the trail.

A large insect whizzed past my head. I swatted at it and urged Dick into a fast walk. Apparently he had stepped on a yellowjacket nest. The angry wasps had counterattacked, stinging the packhorses.

Neil and I pushed our mounts into the forest to gather the packhorses, now out of range of the wasps but still nervous. We led the young packhorses, Crouch and Scarface, back to the trail on their halter ropes. Kit and Rex followed on their own.

As soon as we came to grass we halted. The country around us was low, wet and bushy. We unpacked in a haze of mosquitoes.

We led the horses well away from camp and built four smudge fires for them. There was no direct evidence that smudges had any effect; mosquitoes continued to arrive in multitudes. Nevertheless, the horses stood in the smoke, apparently grateful for it.

"The only sure way of getting rid of mosquitoes is to catch them and break their ribs," asserted Neil.

It took us another day to ride through the mosquito-infested valley of the Kootenay River, across wet meadows and past marshy lakes. Toward the end of the day we reached the Beaverfoot River and followed it to where it forked. The trail forked too. It was a logical place to halt for the night.

At sunup we cooked a large breakfast of bacon and hotcakes. We expected a long day's climb to the top of the pass. The horses assisted in an early start by coming into camp to stand in our campfire smoke.

A set of horse tracks came down one of the forks in the trail, suggesting that somebody had recently crossed the Vermilion Range. There were no tracks on the other trail. The prudent course seemed obvious: take the trail with the tracks.

Near the timberline we came upon a cabin. A young man burst from the door, stopped suddenly and stared. "You guys are different ones," he blurted.

The remark made no sense to me. I asked, "Were you expecting somebody else?"

"Yeah, my partner. He took our horse and went to Golden for grub a week ago. If you saw a drunk in Golden, it was my partner, probly."

"We didn't come from Golden. We came up the Kootenay River. We saw your partner's horse tracks and thought we were on the trail to Lake Louise."

The young man shook his head. "You have went and took the wrong trail. This is where this trail stops. There is no more."

I looked at my watch. It was just past noon. "There is no pass through those mountains ahead, then?"

"Nope, not from here."

Neil said, "It looks like we sweated the horses all morning for nothing."

I looked at the alpine meadow full of herbs and grass. I looked at my watch again. Then I looked at Neil. "We haven't time to get over the mountains today even if we found the right trail. Let's stop here. There's lots of feed for the horses."

The young man broke in. "You can stay in my cabin. But I can't feed you. I am plumb out of grub."

"We have grub," I said.

Neil and I unpacked the horses in front of the cabin, put a bell on Kit and let the animals loose. Then we took the kitchen boxes and our blankets inside.

The cabin had a single window which looked down Moose Creek—the creek we had ascended—to the valley of the Kootenay River. Under the window a table held a few plates and cooking utensils and pieces of rock. Along the other three walls were bunks. In the middle of the room sat a tin stove. The dirt floor was hard and shiny.

We introduced ourselves quickly. "Clifford Kopas."

"Neil Mackay."

"John Britka."

"Let's eat," said Neil.

"I like that idea," smiled John. "I have did hardly any eating for a couple of days." He tossed some twigs and wood into the stove and hovered over them with a match until smoke appeared.

"How about finishing off our eggs and bacon?" I suggested. "They won't last in this hot weather."

"I have some coffee and sugar and porcupine," offered John Britka.

"That is the most interesting menu I ever heard," said Neil. "I will try the porcupine. We have coffee and sugar of our own."

John took a pot from the table and put it on the stove. "It is cooked already. I will heat it up. It is young porky. It tastes something like chicken. Old porky tastes like tree bark and is tough like leather."

After eating, John and Neil fell asleep. John had been up all night trying to trap porcupines, and Neil and I had had little sleep due to the mosquito plague in the Kootenay valley. I resisted my drowsiness and set out to see if we could take our horses over the mountains that rose behind the cabin.

I saddled Dick and rode around the base of Helmet Mountain into an amphitheatre. Cliffs rose on every side, some topped by glaciers. The only way out was the backtrail.

Cumulus clouds, which had been gathering since midmorning, flattened into stratus. Fitful gusts flipped the leaves of alpine plants, creating brief patches of silver on the slopes. The mountains were dull and unattractive. I headed back to the cabin.

I did not disturb the two sleepers. I felt restless. I began to think of this and that and soon settled on food. We had left Wilmer with scarcely enough food to take us to Lake Louise. Now we had lost a day by taking a wrong trail, and to compound the problem, we had discovered a luckless prospector.

Neil and I had a choice to make: either we refused to give John any food or we had to learn how to capture porcupines ourselves.

After supper, John and Neil set up a porcupine trap outside the cabin. It was an empty dynamite box turned upside down and propped up at one end with a stick. Inside the box was a bait of well-salted cooked rolled oats. A string was attached to the trigger stick that held the box up. The string led into the cabin.

John brought out a deck of cards and a cribbage board. He set a candle on the table. The two porcupine trappers were prepared for a night-long vigil. I couldn't keep my eyes open in the warm room. I toppled into my bunk.

Neil Mackay greeting the day in the Rocky Mountains.

The window hinted at dawn when I awoke. The candle was out. I could hear the breathing of Neil and John asleep on their bunks. I arose and peered outside. The dynamite box was still perched on its stick. I put some small pieces of wood on the still living coals in the stove.

Over breakfast, Neil and I estimated how long it would take us to reach Lake Louise. We figured four days.

We packed three days' grub and gave the rest to John Britka. Neil and I were heading into the heart of the Rocky Mountains short on food, the sort of adventure I had once dreamed of.

We dropped quickly down Moose Creek to the forks. There we stopped to tighten cinches and hitches for the long climb up Dainard Creek to Wolverine Pass. Scarface, pestered by mosquitoes, used the pause to try to roll. Before Neil had time to boot her to her feet, a packbox had groaned under her weight.

Climbing through a corridor of long, grey rock walls, we moved toward the timberline. A young moose coming down the corridor stepped aside and stood knee-deep in willows to watch us pass. The horses did not trust him and hurried by.

We topped the summit of Wolverine Pass at sundown. Ahead of us the valley of Vermilion River lay deep in shadow; behind us the valley of the Kootenay was a blue void. Where we were, on top of the high ridge of North America, everything was bathed in pink light.

We rode around the northern shoulder of Mount Gray onto a plateau. Racing with dwindling light, we unpacked at an old camping place. Neil hobbled the horses while I gathered wood from scattered larches.

We awoke in the morning to the crash of falling ice. Tumbling Glacier was living up to its name. Neil sat up in his blankets and stretched. "First time I have heard the break of day."

As the morning advanced, the drone of horseflies was added to the whine of mosquitoes. The large flies bit through clothing and even made attempts on the cowhide-covered packboxes. "The cow has gone," Neil told them.

The horses snorted, shivered and shook their manes. They stood head to tail while we saddled up, the tail of one whisking the face of the other. Once they were saddled we had to watch that they did not try to roll.

It was a shame to leave such a splendid place, but its beauty did not compensate for the harassment of the insects. The horses needed no urging to move out, heading north.

The trail swung along the base of an immense rock wall, over which a mass of ice peered. It dipped into the valley of Helmet Creek and climbed back out. Far to the west on the other side of the mountain, John Britka probably was packing up the last of the food we had given him, preparing for a trip to Golden to find his partner. John would have one day's grub left—just like us.

We camped east of Mount Goodsir. Giving the horses the last of the oats, we turned them loose with only a bell to hold them. They needed plenty of room to graze on the succulent but not very nourishing alpine plants.

In the morning we could neither see our horses nor hear their bell. We assumed the bunch was resting quietly behind a hillock or a patch of trees.

After breakfast we scoured the countryside. We heard imaginary bells from all directions. The gurgle of a rill became a bell; the tinkle of ice falling from a glacier became a bell; even the roar of Goodsir Creek floating up from the valley became a bell.

We chased illusory bells half the day until heavy clouds boiled across the peaks to the west. They spoke menacingly in deep voices. They stabbed at Mount Goodsir with lightning. Neil and I hid under the short branches of alpine firs. The storm drenched us, then rumbled on to attack peaks farther east.

We hurried back to camp to begin the job of drying our gear. We had not put up the tent, having slept under the stars the previous night. Before searching for the horses, we had spread our dew-dampened blankets to catch the sun; they had caught rain instead.

After we had tossed our blankets over small trees to dry, we made an inventory of our grub supply. We found seventeen prunes,

Wolverine Pass.

Neil Mackay leaving Wolverine Pass.

some beans, two cups of cream of wheat, a little sugar, tea, coffee and powdered milk, a can of soup.

"I think we ought to combine porcupine hunting with horse hunting," suggested Neil.

"A good thought," I agreed. "The far side of every clump of trees will have twice the possibility."

In the evening, still without horses or porcupines, we ate beans. Neil pulled out his mouth organ and played *Home Sweet Home* and the *Cowboy's Lament*. I objected.

"I am trying to drown out the sound of the horse bell," he rejoined.

In the early hours I awoke to Neil's voice saying, "Cliff, something is at our gear."

I strained my eyes toward our pile of saddles, bridles, ropes and camp equipment. A canvas bucket topped off a packbox.

Neil slid out of his blankets. He winced across the stones and heather to our stack of firewood and picked up the axe. Then he moved carefully toward the intruder.

A dark mound rustled away. Neil, clad only in underwear, set out in pursuit. The darkness and stony ground slowed him down.

The porcupine reached the nearest larch tree first. It climbed quickly. By the time Neil arrived, the porcupine was clinging to the top.

Neil made the small tree sweep back and forth in a growing arc. The dark form of the porcupine swung across the brightening sky above the northeastern horizon.

After a few minutes Neil stopped. "He has a good grip. I am just giving him a good time," he declared. "I will have to try something else."

He picked up the axe, and in the gathering light, attacked the tree. At each blow the larch shook and the porcupine shuddered. The animal's teeth chattered with fear.

I wished I could photograph the scene: a near-naked man savagely hacking down a tree in which a panic-stricken porcupine awaited its doom against a dawn sky. It was barbarism in silhouette, tragic and heroic. In broad daylight it would have looked ridiculous.

The tree leaned. Neil struck it with one more blow, and it sagged to the earth. Neil raised the axe and brought it down. The porcupine was dead.

"Got him," the hunter crowed. "Porcupine for breakfast."

The porcupine meat would not cook—at least, it would not become tender. We tested it when the sun rose above the eastern peaks. We tested it when the mosquitoes had warmed enough to begin their day's work. We tested it when the horseflies arrived at midmorning. "I still have to sharpen my knife just to get through the gravy," Neil reported.

We added wood to the fire, supported the bucket carefully on the rocks and then set out to hunt for our horses. The porcupine surely would be cooked by the time we returned.

We got back at noon, still without horses but with sharp appetites. "My appetite always speaks up at noon," said Neil. "And today it is hollering."

He peered into the bucket sitting on the coals of the extinct campfire. He chose a piece of meat and gave it a tentative nibble. "My appetite has nothing good to say about this," he sighed, with a regretful shake of his head.

I tried a piece. "It is flavourful," I said. The flavour was tree bark, the texture shredded moccasin.

We cut the meat into tiny pieces and threw it back into the bucket. Then we added our can of vegetable soup. Our theory was that the meat would give the soup body and the soup would give the meat an acceptable flavour. The theory proved to be flawed. We consoled ourselves with a further theory that porcupine meat must have food value even if taste and texture seemed to deny it.

We started for Lake Louise on foot in the morning, taking with us the last of the beans— already cooked—and seventeen prunes.

The trail led down steep switchbacks to Goodsir Creek. The turbid glacial water flowed swiftly over a wide bed, obscuring boulders and holes. At the first crossing we removed our boots and winced across, coming out on the opposite shore with stubbed toes and feet aching from cold.

The trail followed the north bank only a short distance before crossing again. We removed only our boots and waded across in our heavy wool socks. The wool protected our feet a little from both cold and stones, but the current tried to pull our socks off, throwing us off balance.

A little farther on we swapped sides again. This time we left our boots on. The water felt much less cold and our footing more certain.

A pair of logs spanned the Ottertail River just above its junction with Goodsir Creek. On the east bank the trail divided. We faced the same decision that we'd faced on the other side of the Vermilion Range. The previous decision had been wrong and it had cost us a day's travel and half our grub.

Once again we chose the north fork. The farther we went the thicker the windfalls became. After two increasingly difficult miles we had to admit that we were wrong again. We stopped for our noon meal—three prunes each—and then headed back.

The other trail led up McArthur Creek. As we ascended, the mountains seemed to pull the clouds down around themselves. An early evening crept out of them, and they shed a light drizzle.

Neil, in the lead, called back, "It's not the Chateau Lake Louise but it has a roof."

"What has?"

"This cabin."

It was a basic cabin, no more. It consisted of four log walls, a roof and a doorway. It had no door, no windows, no stove, no bed, no table.

"It surely looks good to me," I said.

Neil snorted. "High class language for low class accommodation."

We ate cold beans outside. Then we went inside and lay down on a pile of moss that the previous resident had gathered.

Something drummed on the roof.

"Rain," announced Neil.

"Good thing," I said. "Rainy nights are warmer than clear ones.

We are lucky."

"Anyone could see how lucky we are," exclaimed Neil. "We have just lost six horses; everything we own is sitting in the middle of the Rocky Mountains; we haven't a bean left to eat; and we are going to sleep with our backs for a mattress and our bellies for blankets."

"It is only temporary," I said.

"That is what I intended to say," said Neil. "We are lucky."

I awoke with a start. Something was gnawing on my boot, which was still on my foot. I let out a bellow. The rustle of porcupine quills moved through the grey doorway.

"You useless creature!" I shouted. "You are not even good to eat."

I ran my fingers over my boot. It was undamaged; apparently the animal had awakened me with its first tentative bite.

"Porky only wanted breakfast," Neil pointed out.

"I am hungry enough to eat my boots myself," I retorted.

"Go ahead; they're your boots."

We waited for the day to brighten a little and then started up the trail. It was steep. We expected the exertion to warm us, but our empty bellies did not generate much warmth—or energy.

At the gentle summit of McArthur Pass we rested a few minutes, then continued on, with gravity giving us a push downhill.

We soon arrived at the rear of the Lake O'Hara Chalet. The aroma of bacon and eggs came from an open window. I knocked on the door. A young woman opened it. She surveyed Neil and me from head to toe, taking in our dirty black cowboy hats, dirty bearded faces, dirty slept-in clothes, scuffed riding boots.

"We are pretty hungry . . . " I began.

"You are just in time for breakfast," she said.

Mrs. Greaves sat us down at the kitchen table. A shapely girl with apple cheeks, black hair and bright eyes came and went from the adjoining room with platters of bacon and eggs, hotcakes and toast. Neil and I were stunned by her beauty. After a period of bustle she stopped in the kitchen and acknowledged our presence. "You are guests?" she asked with a European accent.

Neil croaked in an adolescent falsetto he thought he had outgrown, "No." Trying to cover his embarrassment and to hold the beauty's attention, he gushed forth, "We came for help. We lost our horses on the Goodsir Plateau. They made themselves as scarce as bird shit in a cuckoo clock."

Mrs. Greaves chuckled, and the girl said, "That is funny." Neil turned red under his stubble. The two women went into the other room with another load of food.

"I can see why you don't have any luck with girls," I hissed.

"I can't think of anything to talk about any more except horses."

"Why bring a cuckoo clock into it? She is probably Swiss; you may have offended her."

Neil brightened a little. "She said I was funny. She didn't even notice you."

I said, "We are both giddy from the heat in here. I can hardly keep my eyes open."

Roy Greaves entered the kitchen. He grinned at us. "My wife just told me you lads are short on grub and horses."

"That's right," I said quickly, determined to do the talking this time. "Our horses disappeared on the Goodsir Plateau, all six of them. We have to get some grub before we can go back and track them down."

"I'm running my horses in today for a trail ride. I can loan you a couple. But I have only one spare saddle."

Neil and I spent most of the day in the chalet lounge, falling asleep in our chairs. Late in the afternoon a group of mountaineers thumped onto the verandah. The beautiful girl burst from the kitchen and passed through the lounge. She greeted the guide in German.

Was he her husband or father? Neil spotted some grey in his beard. Father, he decided. He went out to the verandah with me in his wake.

"Where did you climb today?" Neil inquired.

"Abbot Pass from Lake Louise." The guide seemed disinclined to talk. This ragged youth was obviously not a mountaineer.

Neil persisted. "How long would it take us to get there?"

"How I would know? How fast you go? I do not know. Maybe you fall in crevasse and never see you again."

Neil and I slunk back to the lounge.

"He is not as nice as his daughter," said Neil.

"How do you know?" I replied. "The only words she's said to you are 'That is funny.' It is Mr. and Mrs. Greaves who are nice; they are going to help us to get back to Goodsir Plateau."

In the morning we went to the corral with Roy Greaves. He picked out a sure mare (sure not to buck) and a not-so-sure gelding. He told us their names, which we promptly forgot. On the trail we renamed them Sure and O'Hara.

I saddled O'Hara and swung into the saddle. Neil slid onto Sure's bare back. Mrs. Greaves handed me two sacks of grub, and I hung them on the saddlehorn. We set out for Goodsir Plateau, a seven-hour ride according to Roy Greaves.

As we approached McArthur Pass, a sudden gust whipped through the defile. Neil was in the lead; his big black hat sailed off, striking O'Hara in the face. The horse reared and came down on his front feet. Taken by surprise, I was nearly thrown. I grabbed for a shorter rein to keep the horse's head up but I was too late.

I found myself on the ground, stunned and bewildered. How had I been thrown so easily? I was no bronc buster but I was not a greenhorn either. Even the horse seemed puzzled; it looked down at me questioningly.

I was still in the saddle. Seeing that I was unhurt, Neil scoffed, "Only a dude would unsaddle his horse before dismounting."

I disentangled my feet from the stirrups and stepped over the offensive hat. I looked at it a moment. Then I picked up a jackpine club. "That's not a hat," I declared. "It's a porcupine." I clubbed the crown flat. Then I picked the hat up and inspected it. "Funny, no quills."

Neil sat on his horse dumbfounded. Then he reined Sure about and charged me. As he went past I handed him his crushed hat on the end of the club.

"Your brain has a loose cinch and a heavy top pack," he barked over his shoulder.

A latigo strap had broken. I repaired it with a saddle string and my jack-knife.

Late in the afternoon we arrived at our campsite. It seemed like a sort of homecoming. I said to Neil, "How about a few bars of *Home Sweet Home*?" then added quickly, "Just kidding!"

We picketed O'Hara and Sure with great care. As I tied the picket rope around O'Hara's fetlock, I said, "If we lose these horses it would be too humiliating to walk to Lake O'Hara again."

Neil agreed. "I would go back to Moose Creek and spend the rest of my life trapping porcupines with John Britka."

In the morning the rising sun set the frosted grass to sparkling. The still air was weighted only with the sound of rushing water. "A good day for horse hunting," I declared.

"There's no need for that," said Neil. "Listen."

I heard the clank of a horse bell. On the ridge behind us six horses appeared. They walked toward us, ears forward. We went out to greet them with kind words in our mouths and halters behind our backs. The horses stopped, reflected on the joys of freedom and trotted off.

Running back and forth across Goodsir Plateau was our crackbrained horses' idea of fun. Neil and I had no choice but to play their game until they tired of it. Eventually they allowed themselves to be pushed between two moraines. By then fatigue and rough ground had reduced everyone to a walk.

After lunch we packed up and travelled quickly over the familiar trail to Lake O'Hara. There was no need to spare the animals; Roy Greaves' horses were without loads, and ours had just had a week-long holiday.

We pulled up at the Lake O'Hara Chalet at dusk, much to the surprise of the people there. For a few minutes I horse-traded with Roy Greaves; I had taken a liking to O'Hara. Greaves said the animal was a spare; he was for sale. If I bought O'Hara, I would have a good string of horses for mountain travel: Dick, Rex, Kit, Crouch and O'Hara. Jimmy and Scarface were Neil's horses.

Next morning Neil and I rode away from Lake O'Hara with seven horses. As we started down the trail toward Kicking Horse Pass, I looked back at our pack string and felt mighty proud. In a few hours we would be back in Alberta with a bigger outfit than we had started with.

At Kicking Horse Pass the trail swung east. We heard steam engines chugging toward the pass not far away.

We came out of the forest with a rush at Lake Louise. Before we had the presence of mind to gather our packhorses together, they had fanned out across the manicured lawns between the Chateau Lake Louise and the lake. The grass was much too short to interest them; they turned their attentions to the flower beds that bordered the lawns. They nipped the heads off flowers as though they had been trained for the job. We had to put Dick and Jimmy onto the artistic landscape in order to remove the packhorses. Horseshoes cut the fragile turf and churned up garden soil. We herded our bunch down to the lakeshore where they could do no more damage.

With our horses gathered on the shore, Neil and I looked furtively back at the big hotel. The picture window overlooking the famous view was lined with spectators. A woman burst from the hotel and ran toward us. My heart sank. How much would the hotel charge us for damaging the lawns and gardens? Would I have to sell O'Hara to pay the bill after owning him for less than a day?

The woman was out of breath by the time she reached us. "That is such a lovely picture with you cowboys and your horses in the foreground, the lake in the centre and the mountains in the background. I do wish the sun was out and there was a boat on the lake. But still it is a most marvellous scene. May I take your picture?"

"Sure," said Neil graciously.

"Surely," said I.

We struck magnificent poses, standing tall in our saddles. The woman was a perfectionist; it took her a long time to frame her picture to her satisfaction. The whole while I expected the hotel manager to sprint down to the lake with the same determination that she had.

Finally. "Click."

"Just one more."

"Click."

"Thank you so much."

"Thank you!" She deserved thanks for recognizing how picturesque and admirable Neil and I were. We were true Rocky Mountain horsemen.

Still expecting to be hauled up by the hotel manager or at least by the gardener, we moved our horses at a fast walk away from the Chateau Lake Louise and down the road.

At the Lake Louise railway station we bought a few groceries, then turned toward Banff. The ride down the Bow Valley was like the ride down the Columbia Valley with some of the heat removed. Passing cars threw up clouds of dust, discouraging Neil from playing his mouth organ. Late in the afternoon we camped twelve miles west of Banff on a meadow backed by the Sawback Range.

The sun was standing tiptoe, peering over the Sawback Range into the Bow Valley, when we started in the morning. We wanted to reach Banff before the tourists were on the move. Riding along boot to boot with the packhorses ahead of us, we planned our day. We would purchase a week's supply of grub at Banff—enough to get us out of the mountains at Sheep Creek where we had come in. Then we would go to a restaurant and order steak with onions.

It was August 8, the height of the tourist season, yet Banff sat quietly in the sun: a tidy, unhurried mountain village. Banff Avenue, the main street, was lined with shops. The shod hooves of our seven horses made a pleasing clop-clop sound on the paved street. We halted in front of a store that sold groceries. Neil stayed outside to tend the horses while I went inside. I came out with the storekeeper, each of us carrying a full cardboard box. I handed my box up to Neil, then mounted Dick. The storekeeper handed me the other box.

With eyes peeled for a place where we could repack our horses, we set off toward the bridge across the Bow River at the edge of town. We could not guide our mounts very well while balancing the boxes of groceries on our saddlehorns. In any case the way ahead was clear, and the few passing motorists slowed courteously.

Suddenly Neil roared, "Scarface, you knothead, come back here!"

I turned to see the young packhorse leaving the string to climb onto the sidewalk. I watched aghast as she walked boldly up to an elderly woman. The woman was panic-stricken. She screamed, "Help! Help! I am being approached! Help!"

Trying to balance his box of groceries on the saddlehorn with one hand, Neil guided Jimmy onto the sidewalk between Scarface and the frightened woman.

I heard Neil blurt out, "I'm sorry, lady. I think the horse is interested in your hat."

The hat was an outsized one designed to protect the lady's delicate skin from the sun at any time of day except sunrise and sunset. It had large floral decorations; the red ones resembled the flowers that the horses had got into at Chateau Lake Louise.

Neil placed a boot against Scarface's jaw and pushed it toward the street. As the filly turned reluctantly, Neil kicked her in the rump and hollered "Git!"

Our packstring moved up Banff Avenue. We passed the restaurant that served steak and onions. We passed Byron Harmon's photographic shop. We crossed over the Bow River bridge. We skirted around the park administration grounds landscaped with enticing flower gardens. Finally we passed some hotsprings stinking of sulphur.

Now well out of town, we were able to set down the boxes of groceries we had been balancing on our saddlehorns for so long. We repacked our horses and moved off again into the heart of the Rocky Mountains. Climbing the western cordillera of North America promised fewer problems than returning to Banff with our horses.

At our campfire beside Sundance Creek I began legal proceedings against Neil for "approaching." He denied the charge

75

and indicted Scarface, who was duly tried and sentenced (in absentia) to a life of hard labour as a packhorse.

The next morning we took the Fatigue Creek trail. It climbed boldly toward the vertical cliffs on the east side of the main stem of the Rockies. Far above the timberline in a high, tilted desert devoid of grass or water, it found a way through the thrusting strata.

With a feeling of relief, we descended to Citadel Pass and camped beside a pond surrounded by grass, a few larches and clumps of alpine fir. Once the horses were attended to, the tent erected and the coffee pot heating, Neil and I annoyed each other in our usual manner: he blew on his mouth organ and I studied maps verbally.

"We are back in British Columbia," I announced.

The mouth organ fell silent. "What?"

"I said we are back in BC."

Neil's face dropped. "Last night you sentenced Scarface to a lifetime as a packhorse. Now it sounds like you have sentenced all of us to crossing the Rocky Mountains between Alberta and British Columbia forever."

The trail took us down from Citadel Pass onto a hillside burnt clean except for snags. Then it levelled out in a narrow valley full of rocks. It was a peculiar valley with no creek and almost no soil. It seemed unfriendly to life. Stunted, scattered spruce and larch struggled to survive in rare pockets of dirt.

We passed a lake sunk far below the level of the valley floor. It had no apparent outlet. It was not so much a lake as an acquisitive depression, receiving water but giving none, too sunken and grudging even to allow its surface to be played upon by a breeze.

It was the first water we had seen for some time. We took the horses down to it. As the animals drank I told Neil about the effect the lake had on my feelings.

He replied, "The water just drains out under the rocks. If you want to deliver a sermon to this lake for being greedy, I will take the horses ahead. I have spent nearly two months trying to reform those horses, and they are as boneheaded as ever. I am not going to try to reform a lake."

Not far from the lake the rocks ended. We broke out onto a broad, grassy meadow. Just beyond it Mount Assiniboine thrust its pyramidal peak into the sky, and a plume of cloud streamed from the summit like a pennant.

Much impressed, I dropped back to ride across the meadow beside Neil. "This is surely the most beautiful place we have seen," I exclaimed.

"It's nice," he replied, revealing an appreciation for mountain scenery unexpressed since Elk Lake.

There was good grass on the bench above Magog Lake at the foot of Mount Assiniboine. We let the horses run loose with a bell, giving even Dick and Jimmy the afternoon off while we explored on foot. We wanted all the horses to be well-rested and well-fed for the long rides we intended to make to complete our journey.

In the morning we rode past the log cabins of Mount Assiniboine Lodge, then through scattered larches in Wonder Pass and finally down the long trail to Bryant Creek. I pointed out to Neil that we were back in Alberta.

At Bryant Creek we turned southeast, crossed the Spray River and rode up its tributary, the Smuts. We moved along doggedly. It was home we wanted now. We had seen the mountains.

At a patch of good grass in the pass near Mud Lake, we pulled the saddles from the horses and set up camp. As we ran the ridge pole through the tent, Neil said, "With any luck, this is the last time we will have to hang this rag over a pole."

The once-white tent was grey and stained. Its roof was pocked with spark holes acquired before we had sense enough to pitch it well away from the campfire. Branch stubs had plucked at it when it was the top pack on a packhorse, leaving right-angled rents.

At dawn I started the campfire in a drizzle. It was easy to do now. The trick was to gather dry twigs in the evening and store them in a canvas bag overnight.

Neil brought in the horses. We saddled them, cinches loose. While the porridge cooked, we struck camp. Ordinarily we left the tent standing until the last moment to allow the sun to dry it. The sun was not at work this day; it had sent rain instead.

We ate breakfast. Then Neil went to the horses and snugged up the cinches. I filled packboxes. To save time—with a twinge of guilt—I packed the porridge pot unwashed.

With teamwork that required scarcely a word, we roped the

Gloria Lake from Wonder Pass.

packboxes to the packsaddles and threw diamond hitches over the loads. We were almost in a spell, as though enchanted by the efficiency we had developed after six weeks in the mountains.

We descended Smith-Dorrien Creek in a downpour. The ranger station at Kananaskis Lakes was only a few hours away. We would soon be dry.

The sight of Kananaskis River was like a prelude to homecoming. "I hope Mackenzie is baking bread today," said Neil as our outfit bunched up at the approach to the packhorse bridge over the river.

We checked the loads. Then I crossed the narrow bridge with Dick. O'Hara, the newest horse in the outfit, was still vying for position. He tried to cross ahead of Scarface who was also a social climber and jealous of her place in the packtrain, Neither horse would give way. They stepped onto the bridge together. O'Hara was heavier than Scarface, but the filly's pack bumped his just as the gelding's hoof slipped off the round brow log.

As he fell from the bridge, the packhorse turned over. He landed in some willows several feet below the bridge, his feet in the air. His pack held him in such a way that he could not regain his feet.

Neil leaped from his saddle and ran down the bank. He tried to pull O'Hara to his feet. He could not move the horse. The pack was wedged between logs left from the bridge construction. Neil undid O'Hara's cinch and pulled the horse to its feet.

I dismounted and went back to inspect my packhorse. He appeared to be unhurt. We let him stand quietly for a few minutes to regain his equanimity. That may have been unnecessary since O'Hara had an abundance of equanimity. Neil called it cussedness.

We repacked O'Hara and led him up the bank to the bridge. I tried to lead him across. He balked. His fall had made him afraid of the bridge. I tugged on the halter rope. O'Hara would not budge. I became exasperated. The rain was soaking everything, even getting inside my slicker and down my neck.

I stopped tugging on the halter rope, tied it in a knot under the horse's chin and strode across the bridge.

"You make him move," I shouted back at Neil.

Neil nudged Jimmy ahead and brought the end of a rope down smartly on O'Hara's rump. The packhorse had not expected that. He started for the bridge and at the last moment ducked to one side. He plunged into the river. The water came up around the packboxes, but the horse did not lose bottom. He emerged on the far side and stood quietly dripping until I fetched him.

Neil asked, "What's in the boxes?"

"Whatever is left of the grub: flour, rolled oats, salt, sugar."

The ranger was not at home and his door was locked. Our dreams of warmth, food and comfort vanished after sustaining us through the long, wet morning. We required new dreams if we were to continue.

I asked Neil, "Shall we camp beside the carved woman or try for Bill Sommers' place at Burns Mine?"

Neil summed up our situation. "It's too miserable to camp here and too far to Burns Mine."

"That's no help," I objected. "We have to be somewhere."

I tried to analyze our situation further. "If we camp here we shall remain wet and miserable— and when we wake up tomorrow morning we shall still be here. If we carry on, we might make it to Bill Sommers' place where we will be dry and fed. The worst that can happen is that we have to camp in the pass, which won't be much worse than camping here."

"Let's go then!" Neil just wanted to do something, anything.

The horses did not welcome the long climb up Pocaterra Creek, particularly O'Hara. He had been shaken by his tumble from the bridge. Besides, it was becoming evident that he believed that Neil and I lacked good sense and that he was going to have to make proper decisions for his own benefit, if not for the entire outfit.

The seven-horse packstring stretched over a fair length of trail. O'Hara chose a position far enough from Neil so that from time to time he was out of sight around a bend. When the trail straightened, Neil noted that a horse was missing. He shouted to me to stop. We backtrailed to find O'Hara hiding in the timber. The second time it happened, two horses were missing. O'Hara was teaching Scarface the trick.

In the rain and drifting clouds, the country at the head of Sheep Creek appeared waxy and unreal. In the lingering evening light the horses became somewhat insubstantial too. O'Hara's behaviour had infected the whole pack string. Every packhorse was trying to sneak off behind the spruce thickets that dotted the high country. They had had enough of the interminable trail.

From out of the dusk a cluster of shacks appeared. A light glowed in the window of one of them.

I shouted back to Neil. "See that light? It's Bill's place."

Neil was too fatigued for enthusiasm. "Yeah, I see it," he replied flatly.

In front of the lighted shack I dismounted stiffly and almost collapsed. Through the uncurtained window I saw Bill Sommers lying on his bunk.

Neil came up with the packhorses. I knocked lightly on the door. There was no response.

"He's asleep," I told Neil.

"Knock louder."

I rapped briskly.

A roar came from the other side of the door. "What the hell you want in the middle of the night? Go away!"

"It's us, Bill," I said to the door.

"It is always us. Us early in the morning, us at noontime, us late in the night. Go away!"

Neil and I were stunned. The man who six weeks earlier had told us we would always be as welcome as the flowers in spring had rejected us; he had told us to go away at a time when we needed food, warmth, shelter and rest as we had never needed them before. There was no doubt about it. We were unwelcome.

I grabbed Dick's reins and led him away. I was too tired to lift myself into the saddle again. Neil was still in the saddle and he pushed the packhorses along behind me.

In a patch of grass below Bill Sommers' shack we slowly pulled the loads and saddles from the horses. The animals did not move after being unsaddled. They just stood with heads drooping. O'Hara sank to the ground with a pathetic groan. Our entire outfit was totally played out.

"I'm too pooped to be hungry," Neil said. "But we have to eat something or we won't have the strength to pull our boots off."

"The grub is in O'Hara's pack," I warned.

It was too dark to see the contents of the packbox. I thrust my hand in blindly. My fingers met dough; everything was covered in wet flour. The paper bag holding the flour had burst.

"If we are not hungry, let's forget about eating," I suggested. "We can't see to rustle firewood even if we had the energy for it."

We did not have the energy to erect the tent either. In any case we could not see to cut tent poles. We spread our blankets on top of wet pack mantles and pulled the tent over us. The rain slacked off a little and we slept.

We awoke to the words, "I am sorry, boys. I did not know it was you last night."

Bill Sommers insisted that Neil and I come to his shack for breakfast. He desperately wanted to atone for his lack of hospitality the previous evening. He explained that in the six weeks since he had seen us many men had come by cadging grub, sometimes stealing it. He had been mulling this over on his bunk when we arrived. My knock had triggered an outburst from a man whose thoughts were already riled.

"That's all right, Bill," said Neil. "We will turn the tables on you. We will give you some grub. It has been preserved by a new method Cliff invented. It is coated with a layer of damp flour to keep it fresh."

I smiled at Neil's attempt to let the old man know that he was as much as ever our friend. Then I looked out the cabin window and broke into a pleased grin. A sense of peace and accomplishment flooded through me. I was looking at seven grazing horses and a pile of gear, worn but in good condition after six weeks in the Rocky Mountains. I felt mighty proud.

INTERLUDE ONE

By the time I was twenty-two I had acquired five horses and a wife. Ruth Hall and I were married in Calgary at noon on June 17, 1933. That very afternoon we started for Bella Coola on the Pacific coast with our horses.

At the outset our saddlehorses were Dick and Rex; our packhorses were Dream, O'Hara and Hash. Hash was too wild for us to handle. In the middle of the Rocky Mountains we traded him to the legendary packer George Rivierre for Peanuts. Peanuts became Ruth's mount; she loved the little horse.

The execrable Goat River Trail between the upper Fraser River

Cliff and Ruth Kopas with Rex, Dream, O'Hara and Peanuts at Quesnel, starting for Bella Coola, September 16, 1933. Photo by Louis LeBourdais.

and Barkerville killed Dick, confirming the wisdom of a horseman who had told me that mountains are too hard on blooded horses. I should have been riding a cayuse. Rex became a saddlehorse again: mine, this time.

From Quesnel we rode up the Blackwater River Valley, following the path of Alexander Mackenzie, my hero. On October 7 we looked into the Bella Coola Valley from the top of the Burnt Bridge Trail. "What a gorgeous gully!" Ruth exclaimed. We liked Bella Coola enough to stay.

I wrote a book about our trip called *Packhorses to the Pacific*.

Nusatsum Mountain and the Bella Coola Valley— the "gorgeous gully"— from the Burnt Bridge Trail.

HOUSE CALL TO THE ULKATCHO CARRIER

"And immediately the spirit driveth him into the wilderness."

Mark 1:12

Mary Jane Jack and Sadie Cahoose at Ulkatcho, August 26, 1934.

HOUSE CALL TO ULKATCHO 1934

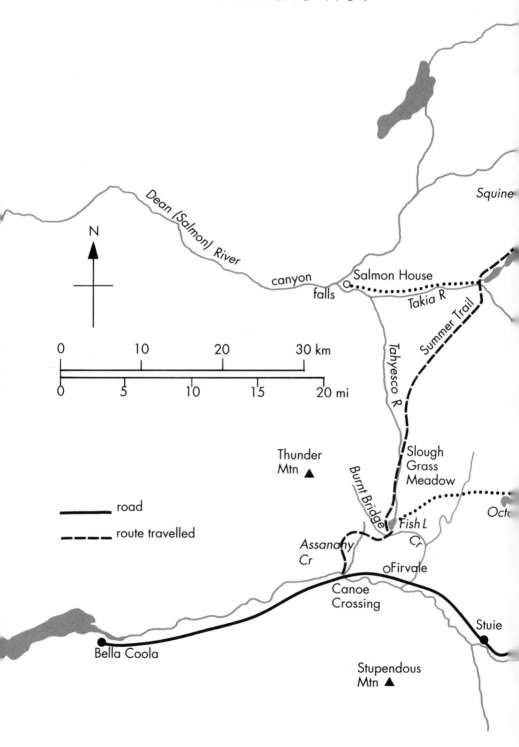

N

0   10   20   30 km

0   5   10   15   20 mi

Dean (Salmon) River

canyon

falls

Salmon House

Takia R

Tahyesco R

Summer Trail

Squine

Thunder
Mtn ▲

Slough
Grass
Meadow

Octo

Burnt Bridge

road

route travelled

Assanany
Cr

Fish L
Cr

oFirvale

Canoe
Crossing

Stuie

Bella Coola

Stupendous
Mtn ▲

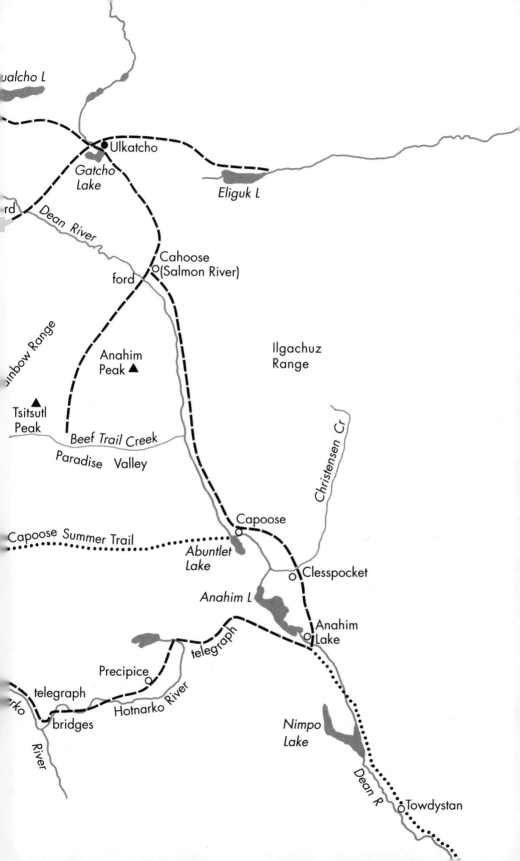

A YEAR AFTER RUTH AND I ARRIVED in Bella Coola we were offered jobs on a horseback expedition to Ulkatcho. It was a chance to earn some money doing what we knew best, which was packhorsing. We needed the money. My winter's work, a manuscript about our packhorse trip from Alberta to Bella Coola, lay in a box, unfavoured by editors. Two of our horses, Rex and O'Hara, had kept us in groceries by offering themselves for sale, along with their rigging.

Early in August 1934 we rode our two remaining horses, Dream and Peanuts, twenty miles up the Bella Coola Valley to Canoe Crossing. Three horses belonging to Tommy Walker at Stuie Lodge and eight from here and there in the valley and the Chilcotin completed the packhorse outfit we were putting together.

In the evening of August 16, Dr. Herman McLean, the doctor at the Bella Coola United Church Hospital, nurses Mary Munn and Ivy Whitmore, and fourteen-year-old Ingraham Harestad arrived by car. The medical packhorse trip to the Stick Indians at Ulkatcho was Dr. McLean's idea. The previous year he had convinced the United Church Board of Home Missions and the Department of Indian Affairs that the only effective way to give the Ulkatcho Carrier Indians medical care was to do it on their own ground. Even though the seminomadic Ulkatchos often rode to Bella Coola, they generally avoided the hospital for the compelling reason that people were known to die there.

The two young nurses were from the Bella Coola Hospital staff. They were volunteers; month-long packhorse trips into Indian country were not demanded of registered nurses even at Bella Coola. Relief medical staff filled the doctor's and nurses' jobs at the hospital while they were away.

Ingraham Harestad was a bright lad from a farm near where Ruth and I had wintered in Lower Bella Coola. His family had recently moved from Kwatna Inlet on the outer coast. He knew boats better than horses. His job would be camp chores.

I watched the newcomers take their personal gear from the car, assessing how it would complete the packs. Ruth and I had already filled most of the packboxes with food and equipment, ready for an early start in the morning.

Dr. McLean brought a duffle bag, a black medical satchel, a Bible and a .30–.30 rifle to the tent he and Ingraham would share.

"What's the rifle for?" I inquired.

"Good hunting on top," the physician replied tersely.

"I wouldn't have packed so much grub if I'd known we'd have a hunter among us."

"The season doesn't open 'til the first of September. We'll eat what you've brought and then kill something and put the meat on the empty packhorses. On our trip last year I saw lots of moose and mowitch and didn't have a gun. It was extremely frustrating."

"What's a mowitch?"

"Deer—a Chinook word everyone uses in this country."

I revived the campfire to make tea. Dr. McLean used the occasion to make a little speech. "I believe God has called me to serve dark-skinned people," he said. "When I was a boy in Manitoba I hoped to follow the example of David Livingstone and go to Africa as a missionary. Instead God has called me to Bella Coola; and indeed there are swarthy people here. This is a Christian expedition. We shall rest on Sunday. There will be no swearing at packhorses as seems to be the custom in this country. We have been instructed not to proselytize; the Roman Catholic Church provides religious instruction to the Interior Indians. We shall demonstrate our faith through our deeds as God directs us in James' epistle: 'Be ye doers of the word and not hearers only. Faith without works is dead.' Now, before we retire to our tents, I would like to say a prayer asking God's blessing on our expedition."

I had never started a packhorse trip with a prayer before. Usually I prayed only at river crossings.

In our tent Ruth asked me, "Who was James?"

"He wrote the Bible."

"I thought God did."

"Well, God had the idea, but James got the words down."

Shouting and a car horn awoke me.

"What time is it?" I asked Ruth, who owned our watch.

"Five after five."

"The doctor seems to want a very early start. We'd better get a move on. The horse wrangler and cook are supposed to be up first."

Even with hobbles, Tommy Walker's three horses had drifted several miles up the road toward Stuie. The other horses had stayed close to camp but didn't want to return to it. Driving horses that don't know each other is like driving a herd of house flies; they go off in all directions. I almost broke Dr. McLean's injunction against swearing.

I tied the horses to trees at the edge of camp beside our pile of saddles and saddle blankets. After breakfast the doctor took Ingraham aside to teach him how to saddle a saddlehorse. I started to saddle the seven packhorses. The nurses volunteered to help Ruth wash dishes and fill packboxes.

Mary Munn set out for the Bella Coola River with a bucket. She stepped over a dead Douglas fir log onto a yellowjacket wasp nest. Yellowjackets are remarkably irritable.

The nurse sprinted for camp screaming, "I'm being stung! I'm being stung!"

On her way to the presumed safety of her tent, she headed toward the doctor who was about to show Ingraham how to place a saddle blanket on Pinto. Consequently the doctor had a blanket open, ready to receive the nurse. He threw it over her head and shoulders.

The wasps under the blanket were bewildered; those outside looked for another target. Ingraham's horse was readily available. The horse reared. Ingraham caught the reins. Then, following the doctor's example, he grabbed a saddle blanket and tossed it over the horse's head. The blinded animal backed into the nurses' tent. The support poles and ridge pole collapsed. The horse's feet became entangled in canvas and clothing. The animal panicked, tore the reins from Ingraham's hands, tossed the blanket from its head, kicked a set of red flannelette pyjamas from its feet and galloped down the road.

Surveying the damage, Dr. McLean asked the boy, "Ingraham,

don't you know the difference between a woman and a horse?"

"No, I don't," replied the boy. "I'm only fourteen."

Shortly before noon, fifty-two horseshoes thumped across the planks of Canoe Crossing Bridge to the foot of Canoe Crossing Trail. I led the cavalcade, followed by the seven packhorses. Ruth rode behind the packhorses to watch for trouble with the loads. Ingraham came last so that he could shoot at fool hens—spruce grouse—with his slingshot.

The Canoe Crossing Trail wound back and forth across the face of the mountain, seeking places between cliffs where horses could find footing. It was steep and unrelenting. Facing south, it was hot too. The horses moved slowly and rested often.

I heard a scream two switchbacks below me. The trail was very steep at that point. I dismounted and squeezed past the packhorses. Ruth was not in her saddle, nor was Dr. McLean. I came to the white saddlehorse called Cream. Behind the horse, Dr. McLean appeared to be removing Mary Munn's clothes. Ruth looked on, as did Ivy Whitmore.

"What happened?"

Ivy Whitmore spoke. "Mary's horse lunged to get up that steep place and something broke. The saddle slid over the end of the horse with Mary in it."

The doctor added, "I believe the saddle mitigated the impact. No broken bones. A large contusion, though."

The injured nurse sat at the edge of the trail. "First wasps, now this," she whimpered.

"Bad luck," I said.

"We should thank God that you are not allergic to wasps and that the saddle broke your fall," said Dr. McLean.

The doctor and I repaired the broken cinch. With our assistance Mary climbed back into the saddle. The packtrain moved forward again slowly.

Gaps appeared in the forest. We drew our horses together at an opening that overlooked the Bella Coola Valley. On the valley bottom the river wove a broad silver cord through a green carpet.

Silver threads joined it from the south; above them glaciers hung on mountain walls. Waterfalls flung themselves from cliffs. The hiss and roar of falling water grew and waned as convection currents of air rose fitfully from the valley.

Mary Munn gazed at the scene for several minutes and then passed judgement on her calamitous day. "The view alone is worth it!" she declared.

The trail eased over a shoulder of the mountain and flattened out. We unpacked beside a small lake. There was more mountain above us, but we'd had enough of it for one day.

The horses were so fatigued that they did not move after being unsaddled. They stood rooted to the ground, heads hung low. The rest of us felt listless, too, except for Dr. McLean who went for firewood.

Eventually the horses moved off to graze, and we gathered enough energy to prepare a meal. After eating we searched the sky and agreed that it held no rain. We were too tired to set up tents. We unrolled our sleeping bags under trees at the edge of the meadow and erected canopies of mosquito netting.

At dawn I could hear the bell on Dream. Nevertheless, I got up to count horses. Sure enough, three were gone: Tommy Walker's three aristocrats. I found hoofprints on the backtrail and soon caught up to the feet that made them. Horses are twilight travellers; I was grateful that these horses had chosen morning twilight rather than evening twilight to pull out. Otherwise I might have had to climb the Canoe Crossing Trail again.

We had made such a rudimentary camp the previous evening that we had little to pack in the morning. We were on the trail by nine o'clock. We climbed through patches of alpine trees in the headwaters basin of Assanany Creek toward seemingly impassable bluffs.

The trail followed the creek and then swung suddenly along the base of the bluffs, climbing. The horses picked their way over gravel and rocks, up patches of snow and across bare granite. At the top the trail traversed a narrow ledge above high cliffs. It sneaked around seemingly impassable shoulders of rock on the very rim of the Bella Coola Valley and then swung away to skirt narrow canyons.

We walked, leading our mounts, trusting more in the grip of our bootsoles than in steel horseshoes on gravel-scattered bedrock. We would have walked anyway on such a steep slope to save our horses' strength.

At the high point of the trail we halted for a photograph. We were well above the timberline. Wind-flattened fir and whitebark pine cowered in hollows between glacier-scraped knolls. Far below, the Bella Coola River sent up a low roar from its riffles. A diminutive bridge spanned the river, the one we had crossed the previous morning. In one day we had travelled a mile—vertically.

The sky had become overcast and the wind cold, but the scenery was grand. Ahead of us the trail led across alpine country over gentle slopes, as though atoning for the punishment it had given us on the way up from Canoe Crossing.

We saw Fish Lake five miles ahead just before we descended

Ruth Kopas, Dr. Herman McLean, Mary Munn, Ivy Whitmore and Ingraham Harestad at the summit of the Canoe Crossing Trail.

into the forest. We splashed across Burnt Bridge Creek and climbed over a ridge to the lake.

Fish Lake was the junction of the Canoe Crossing Trail, Burnt Bridge Trail, Capoose Trail and the Ulkatcho Summer Trail (or Slough Grass Trail). It was a popular camping place; the numerous tethering pickets in the swamp meadows indicated that. So did the cropped grass. We decided to move on to the big meadow at Slough Grass, hoping for better horse feed.

Ingraham was disappointed. He had seen dozens of rainbow trout swimming lazily in the clear, shallow water of Fish Lake. Two grouse had fallen to his slingshot already. He wanted to live off the land.

At five o'clock we reached Slough Grass Meadow, delighted to see that it offered more than its name suggested, which was a dry camping place with adequate horse feed. It had beauty and even drama. Over the ridge to the west Thunder Mountain loomed and boomed, hung with glaciers that occasionally broke loose to give the mountain its name. To the south, the circular snow- covered summit of Stupendous Mountain beamed like a small moon. We were on the western slope of the Rainbow Mountains, but their legendary beauty was hidden by dark forest.

A missionary packtrain does not travel on Sunday. In any case we all needed rest. I was mortified to discover that Tommy Walker's three horses had saddle sores. Their packsaddles did not fit their backs.

Dr. McLean spent the day in his tent; Ingraham reported that he was reading the Bible. Ingraham gathered firewood and then asked if I would teach him how to pack a horse.

We took a halter to the meadow and led Bluey back to camp. The horse walked to the campfire and straddled it, to the annoyance of the women. The horses were being tormented by sandflies and mosquitoes. Bluey was a wise old animal who knew the repellent qualities of woodsmoke.

I started the lesson. "First, put two saddle blankets on his back, well forward. The bars of the saddle will fit just behind his shoulder blades where there is lots of movement of muscles and hide. If the blankets slip back, he will soon have a sore. Set the packsaddle on the blankets behind the withers. Reach under his belly for the cinch and pull tight with the latigo. Hook up the breast collar; then put the breeching under his tail. They keep the saddle from sliding back or ahead on steep hills. Put the packboxes in the basket ropes and tie them down. The boxes must be of equal weight or a sore forms on the light side. Put the pack cover over the load, then throw the lash cinch across the load and snug it down with the lash rope in a diamond hitch. Once you begin the diamond hitch never give slack."

We packed and unpacked Bluey twice with empty packboxes. The old horse must have wondered at the interminable cinching and tugging, the saddling up and unsaddling without going anywhere. He stood patiently wherever the campfire smoke was. Ingraham had learned how to pack empty boxes but he probably was not strong enough to lift full eighty-pound packboxes to the packsaddle and tie them on. The doctor and I would still have to do the packing.

Early Monday morning, twelve horses stood on the frosted meadow. One horse was missing. I checked the trail for tracks both back and ahead. I inspected the edge of the meadow where a horse might stand quietly behind trees. I even reminded myself of the story of a wrangler who was one horse short and hunted all day for the missing animal until somebody pointed out that he was riding it.

Back at camp I remarked, "Thirteen is surely an unlucky number. Once before, I started out with thirteen horses and lost one the first night."

"You are superstitious," Dr. McLean responded. "You should pray about it. I shall pray too. I am sure the hand of God is in this, and it will prove providential."

I said despondently, "I won't pray for myself but I may send up a few words for the horses. Some of them are already sore-backed and now they have to share the load of the lost horse."

In the brief prayer that preceded breakfast, Dr. McLean mentioned both the horse and me.

The others went ahead while I stayed back to search for the

horse. Eventually I gave up. I had hoped that the horse would want to stay with the others. Instead, it was Dream who sent up a shrill whinny of distress when we returned to the vacated camping place.

I overtook the outfit in a tangle of windfalls. I was welcomed warmly and handed an axe. Once through the timber, we encountered a bog. Dream went down on her side in the quagmire. I stepped from the saddle and slogged to firm ground on foot, followed by my horse throwing mud from her hooves. The others dismounted; people and horses all chose their own way across.

We went over a rocky ridge, a ghostly place of grey fire-killed lodgepole pine, and descended to another bog in the middle of which a small, mud-bottomed creek flowed sullenly. Logs had been laid across it but they were of no use to horses. Despite the example of the other horses, the grey, an independent thinker, refused to come across. I had to put a rope around her neck, wrap a dally around Dream's saddlehorn and pull the reluctant packhorse across.

We forded two wide, clear streams that flowed from the Rainbow Mountains and then left the high country behind. Ahead was a broad plateau covered with spruce and lodgepole pine, opening here and there to wide meadows and lakes. At the lakes were Ulkatcho Indians, our prospective patients.

At the Takia River, near the outlet of the Tanya Lakes, we joined the trail that ran between Salmon House Falls on the Takia River and Ulkatcho. We halted and set up camp. We would find patients at Tanya Lakes.

The doctor unpacked his black bag and medicines. "This will be the site of the first clinic," he declared. He held his hands out for water as though preparing for an operation. He was a serious man but not humourless. No water was forthcoming. "You will have to wash for supper in the creek like the rest of us, doctor," Ivy Whitmore laughed.

Our campfire smoke and grazing horses disclosed our presence to others. An Indian boy about twelve years old soon showed up. He wore moosehide moccasins, a cap, cotton trousers too long for him and a ragged shirt held together by a single large white button.

He studied us silently for a moment, then spoke to Dr. McLean. "Papa yaka papa ticky doctin. Nika sick kopa tooth."

"Tomolla," replied Dr. McLean.

The boy left.

"What did he say?" asked Mary Munn.

"He said his grandfather wants to see a doctor; he has a bad tooth."

"And what did you say?"

"Tomorrow. I have picked up a little Chinook since I arrived in Bella Coola five years ago—the easy words. Much of Chinook is from English and French but altered because the Indians cannot pronounce F and R. A missionary should be able to speak the language of the people he serves."

"How did the Indians know we were medical people?"

"Moccasin telegraph. News travels fast where there are few people. Word left Bella Coola before we did."

The doctor roused us half an hour later than usual; there was no point in getting up before our patients. Fog covered Tanya Lakes and crept across the meadow and into the trees. Coyotes barked at the edge of the meadow.

"I'd like the hide of one of those blighters," exclaimed the doctor. He picked up his rifle and strode away across the dew-soaked swamp.

"I hope he doesn't mistake a horse for a moose in the fog," I said. "We are already short a horse."

The doctor returned soon without a shot fired. Evidently his sense of professional duty had overcome his passion for hunting.

After breakfast I accompanied the doctor and nurses to the Indian camp. A structure appeared through the trees, a startling shape in the wilderness. It was an open shed roofed with spruce bark. Salmon hung from the beams. Smoke from a campfire drifted up to them. Stacks of dried salmon were piled here and there. A tent had been erected under one end of the shed. Another smokehouse and several tents stood nearby.

"Klahowya," Dr. McLean called loudly.

Emaciated Ulkatcho Indian man in spark-holed tent at Tanya Lake.

The boy of the previous evening emerged from a tent, followed by a girl a little younger and a woman. Finally an old woman came out. She looked at us and then screamed shrilly toward a small tent.

Dr. McLean went to the tent and looked in. I was right behind him. We were white people; we could go where we liked and look into anything.

The doctor recognized the man in the tent. "Klahowya, Cahoose," he said.

An emaciated old man with tousled hair, scraggly beard and filmed eyes sat on the ground beside a tin heater. A stove pipe went through the spark-holed canvas roof.

"Chako klahani. Come outside," said the doctor and backed out.

We directed the little group of Stick Indians to a corner of one of the smokehouses where there was a boulder to serve as a table. Dr. McLean set his medical instruments on the boulder. He and nurse Whitmore wore white surgical smocks. Otherwise the doctor's costume was unorthodox for medical work: leather boots, puttees kept from his service in the Great War, breeches and a cloth cap.

Dr. McLean inspected ears, eyes and teeth. He knew that old Cahoose was in the terminal stage of pulmonary tuberculosis. He knew, too, that there was nothing he could do to alleviate it, nor could he prevent its spread to others. The government would not provide money for chronic care, and even if it did, the Indians would flee the hospital.

Dr. McLean said, "The boy, the girl and old Cahoose have dental caries. Each of them requires an extraction. The white man's gifts to these people are white sugar and the white plague. Beware that they do not give their gift to us."

"What would that be?" asked Ivy Whitmore cautiously.

"Pediculosis."

Dr. McLean lifted the lapel of the boy's jacket. The cloth was white beneath with lice and nits.

"An extreme case of pediculosis," observed the doctor. "The Indians accept lice as an unavoidable part of life—like mosquitoes in summer and cold in winter. The children have their own remedy: they eat their tormentors." He picked a louse from the boy's jacket and said "muckamuck." The boy complied, snapping the louse between his front teeth.

"I don't want to see any more of that," said the nurse.

"Let's get down to business," said Dr. McLean. "I cannot cure tuberculosis or pediculosis. The close, unsanitary way these people live ensures that the diseases will spread. But tooth decay can be stopped by removing the tooth." He looked at the boy. "You first."

The boy stood in moccasined feet beside the fish-drying shed. The doctor grasped a tooth in the boy's lower jaw with forceps and twisted and pulled. Standing behind the lad, Ivy Whitmore held his head steady. The boy groaned. The tooth came free and the doctor held it up like a trophy.

"Delate skookum tumtum," he praised the boy. "Very brave."

He said to me, "Cliff, go to camp and bring back some cornmeal. I don't want these people eating fish or moose meat today."

By the time I returned, the doctor had extracted a tooth from the girl—a few tears were shed in that operation evidently. The next patient was old Cahoose. He sat on the ground, leaning against the boulder to support himself.

"Nika waum sick," he told the doctor.

"Of course you have a fever, Cahoose. You have tuberculosis and Rigg's disease. The bacteria from the abscess in your gums may have entered your blood."

"Tell him to come to the hospital in Bella Coola," suggested Ivy Whitmore. "While he is there we could burn his clothes and get rid of his lice." She was not comfortable touching lousy patients.

"He would not live long in the hospital," replied the doctor. "He might as well live out his life here, difficult as it is. This hard country is his home."

Old Cahoose's tooth was already loose; it came free readily. Pus ran from the gums. Cahoose spat blood and pus onto the ground.

"No wonder he is sick," remarked Ivy Whitmore.

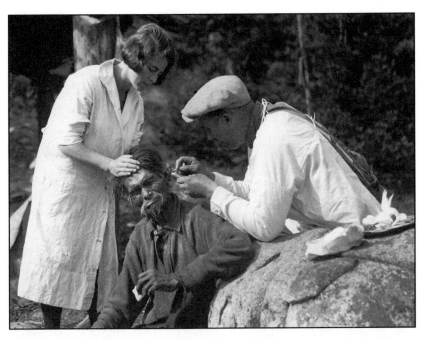

Dr. Herman McLean and Ivy Whitmore inspect Old Cahoose's ear.

Salhkus, wife of Chantyman, at the Tanya Lake fish drying camp.

Dr. McLean vaccinated the girl and the boy for whooping cough, then looked at his watch. "Cracky, it's only noon. We have time to get to Squiness Lake."

My heart sank. We had planned to stay the day in the expectation that the strayed packhorse would rejoin our bunch. I also wanted the saddle sores on Tommy Walker's horses to have time to close up a little.

I asked, "What about the Indians fishing at Salmon House Falls west of here? Aren't you going to doctor them?"

"Oh, they will learn by moccasin telegraph that we have gone to Ulkatcho. They have to pack dried salmon home anyway." He paused, perceiving the intent of my question. "If you are worried about the packhorse, pray about it. Jesus said in the gospel according to Matthew, "Whatsoever ye shall ask in prayer, believing, ye shall receive."

Back at camp I complained to Ruth, "That doctor is a driver."

Ruth pointed out, "He is also the boss. Anyway, the trail from here on is mostly level and dry, if I remember it right."

The trail was indeed good, but the hot afternoon brought horseflies and sandflies. Late in the afternoon we unpacked at Squiness Lake in a storm of flies. I felt sympathy for the horses; they shook their heads, snorted, stamped and swished their tails in a constant struggle with the insects. I tethered and hobbled them all. I was afraid they might leave the country in an attempt to escape the flies.

Our own battles with the insects so tired and demoralized us that we did not have the energy to set up a good camp. Ingraham gathered firewood, Ruth and the nurses cooked supper, and then everyone sought the imperfect shelter of their mosquito netting and blankets.

In the morning the meadow was white with frost. Mist licked the surface of Squiness Lake. There were no insects; they were somewhere out of sight, torpid with cold. Their absence gave us a sense of freedom and energy. We were packed and away at eight-thirty, an unbelievably early start.

I led the packtrain at an easy pace, enjoying the long corridor through the forest, confident that there would be no problems. The trail we were travelling was one of the most heavily used in the country.

Without the diversion of bog holes and periodic bushy detours, the riders tired of the monotonous plod. Ivy Whitmore fell asleep and fell out of the saddle when her half-asleep horse stumbled on a log. The nurse was unhurt but had to bear jibes about her riding ability. Ingraham, spotting two fool hens, tied the reins to Pinto's saddle and took off on foot with his slingshot. The grouse flew from perch to perch, leading the boy through the woods in a wild grouse chase. Fool hens are not smart but they are good duckers. Ingraham caught up with the rest of us at the Dean River ford without grouse and low on self-confidence as a hunter. He had lost his moosehide gauntlets.

Mary Jane Jack at Ulkatcho.

The Ulkatcho Catholic church and cemetery.

On the east side of the Dean River, the country ran more to meadows. Dr. McLean rode off the trail from side to side searching for patients putting up hay. Time and again he crossed moose tracks. "I smell game," he told me excitedly.

As we ascended from Dean Meadows we met two Indian children. They led us to an Indian camp at the edge of a hay meadow. The doctor and Mary Munn stayed behind while the rest of us pushed on to Ulkatcho.

We crossed the creek at the outlet of Gatcho Lake, climbed a short hill and emerged from the poplar and spruce trees onto a sloping, clover-covered meadow crowded with grave houses. We continued through the deserted village of Ulkatcho to a meadow at the east end of Gatcho Lake where we set up camp.

Dr. McLean and Mary Munn arrived in time for supper. The nurse was much relieved to see us. She had feared a night in the wilderness without tent or blankets.

Immediately after supper I told Dr. McLean that I was worried about our galled packhorses. I pointed out that we had put in long days with heavy packs on rough trails on the first two days of the trip. That is when the sores had started. Then we had lost a horse which resulted in heavier loads for the remaining packhorses. I explained that the kidney bars on Tommy Walker's packsaddles did not fit his high-withered horses. In fact the new sores were on proud flesh of old sores.

Dr. McLean said, "Tommy Walker is a green Englishman," as if that resolved the problem.

In the dusk, the empty cabins and the grave houses on the hill above us intensified the desolation of the dark, forested country. Loons uttered weird cries on Gatcho Lake. On a hill northeast of us a wolf moaned, then a chorus of howls arose.

"Why would anyone live at a place like this?" asked Mary Munn.

Dr. McLean answered. "I don't know. But they do, and we are going to stay four days to serve them. We have been in the country long enough for word about us to spread. In a day or two the Indians in outlying fishing and haying camps will be here. The Indians are familiar with the procedure. In June they gather at Ulkatcho for priest time. This will be doctor time."

Dr. McLean and the nurses set out early in the morning for Captain Harry's place at Qualcho Lake. Ingraham and I tethered the horses to new pickets. I hated to tether the horses; they could feed and fight flies better when unconstrained. But I dared not risk having them move out on us.

Ruth and I wanted some time to ourselves. We set Ingraham to baking bannock. The recipe of three cups of flour, two teaspoons of baking powder and a little salt mixed with water into thick dough was easy to follow. The challenge was to get the sticky dough off your hands into a frying pan and bake it into palatable bread. I told the boy, "Prop the frying pan in front of the fire, not on it. Bannock is best baked, not fried. It should be a cross between a tired baking powder biscuit and a puffed-up hotcake. The closer you get to the baking powder biscuit the better. Wash your hands before you mix the dough. Horse sweat does not qualify as salt."

Then I said to Ruth, "Let's get out of here. In a few minutes there will be dough stuck to everything."

We climbed the hill to Ulkatcho. The church, built of hand-sawn lumber, was imposing in the little village of small log cabins. Inside, it was a retreat from the sombre wilderness. The chancel contained an incense burner and six large candles flanked by plaster statuettes of Mary and Joseph, each holding an infant.

"Evidently Jesus was twins," I observed. "I shall have to tell Dr. McLean."

"You will not!" Ruth exclaimed. "We are on this trip to earn money, not to engage in religious controversy."

We looked into houses too. They were dirty and almost devoid of furniture, but two had spring beds, one a phonograph, another a radio and one a violin hanging on a wall. In the darkness of a decrepit cabin we came face to face with a wrinkled old woman dressed in dark clothes. We were abashed, knowing ourselves to be snoops. The old woman thought I was the doctor. "Lametsin, lametsin," she cried. She rubbed her hands. On the window sill sat an empty bottle of Absorbine Jr.

I said to Ruth, "Go back to camp and see if you can find pain reliever in the hospital box. Now that we have barged in on the old lady, we should be gracious to her. I'll try to get a photograph."

Ruth returned with a small tin of yellow oxide of mercury ointment. We had no idea of what it was for. I told the old woman to rub it on her skin. It probably would do no harm.

Dr. McLean and the nurses rode into camp after dark, very tired. Ingraham's bannock took the edge off their hunger, hard crusts and raw centres notwithstanding. The nurses had a wonderful tale of cute Indian youngsters on horseback guiding them back to Ulkatcho. Tiny moccasined feet had vibrated against the horses' flanks, urging them on. Through mudholes and over rocky ridges, on trail and off, smiles flashed back at the white people at every difficulty overcome.

"By the way," I asked irrelevantly, "What is yellow oxide of mercury used for?"

"It is a mild antiseptic for application to the eyelids," replied Dr. McLean.

Dr. McLean was up at six-thirty in the morning. He was tireless.

He and I saddled Dream and Dan and put a pack on Pinto.

The doctor said to Ingraham, "Cliff and I are going east to Eliguk Lake overnight. You will stay here and look after the horses and women. You are old enough to handle the job and young enough to be above suspicion."

The trail east of Ulkatcho was actually a wagon road, although one would scarcely guess it. Wagons in the Ulkatcho country were built narrow in order to thread through the jackpine and spruce forests. Roads built for them required the removal of few trees.

About noon we spotted a rider ahead, then a wagon and team. The rider was Indian, the teamster white.

"White people!" exclaimed the teamster with a Scottish accent. "The country is becoming nigh infested with them. I heard that the policeman from the Chilcotin is coming, and now a doctor. We only just got rid of the priest in June."

"Well, what are you, then?" demanded Dr. McLean.

The teamster cracked a reluctant smile. "I am John Ward, a white man, also a trader, Paul Krestinuk's partner. He built this excuse for a wagon road—two hundred miles of rocks, stumps, mudholes and downed trees all the way from Quesnel. Where are you headed?"

"To Captain Alexis'."

"This gentleman with me is Captain Alexis."

"Klahowya," said Dr. McLean.

"Hello. I talk English," said the Indian.

The teamster said, "There are people at Eliguk Lake who are expecting you." He snapped the lines across his horses' backs and started ahead slowly, explaining, "I want to get to my store. I have been on the trail two weeks."

As we rode along, I said to Dr. McLean, "I am puzzled by the captains we hear about in this plateau country, like Captain Harry and Captain Alexis. I have yet to see a boat."

"Ask the trader when we get back to Ulkatcho."

At noon we dismounted for lunch. Dr. McLean tied Dan some distance from Dream and Pinto. Dan would not eat.

John Ward, the trader at Ulkatcho.

"Horses are just like men," observed the doctor. "They won't eat on account of females. Isn't it a corker when dumb animals get as crazy as men on account of women."

Early in the afternoon we came to an Indian fishing camp at the outlet of Eliguk Lake. Trout were drying on racks over slow fires. Two men were cutting long, narrow strips from a tanned moosehide. Two women were braiding moosehide ropes.

The Indians were fully occupied with their work. They seemed indifferent to us. They had heard that a doctor was coming, so one by one they were gracious enough to permit a brief medical examination on the spot. Then they went back to work. They appeared to be in good health.

The ride to Eliguk Lake had been unnecessary, but Dr. McLean did not care. His image of himself as a missionary required relentless activity. It was the effort that mattered. After we had bedded down at dusk, he said, "Sleeping in horse blankets under the stars—who would not want to be a doctor?"

We reached our camp at Gatcho Lake in midafternoon the next day. The women and Ingraham were at the lake. The doctor and I joined them on the rocky beach.

The women looked as clean as scraped carrots. Obviously they had bathed, probably in a basin in the privacy of their tents. Wishing more scope for her ablutions, Ivy Whitmore had ingeniously fashioned a swimming costume from a towel, a few pins and a cord over her shoulders. She waded into the warm water and made a shallow dive. She came up with a heavy, sagging swim suit. Towels

Cliff Kopas, Ivy Whitmore (in swimsuit made from a towel), Ingraham Harestad, Dr. Herman McLean and Mary Munn on the beach at Gatcho Lake.

are designed to absorb a lot of water quickly.

"Keep your eyes open and you will learn about women," I told Ingraham.

He shrugged self-consciously.

The nurse waded ashore, grasping desperately at the cloth as the pins and shoulder strap pulled free. The waterlogged towel resumed its rectangular shape, covering the woman's front, but abandoning her backside to our admiring stares. The nurse headed for camp as fast as bare feet on stony ground would permit.

Ruth and I walked to the small log store at the edge of Ulkatcho village. Three old Stick Indians were there to see what the trader had brought from Quesnel in his wagon. We introduced ourselves to the trader, John Ward, and he introduced us to Stillas, Sundayman and Chantyman.

"The boys are pretty well lit up on soapallalie wine," said the trader. "They are telling stories about hyas ahnkutte, old times."

Sundayman was relating his memories of the Canadian Pacific Railway survey that went through Ulkatcho country in 1876. He remembered Hunter and Seymour and the hunchbacked geologist George Dawson. "Yahka hyiu tikegh iskum chickamin stone," said Sundayman.

"He wanted rocks with minerals in them," translated the trader.

Sundayman told a story about the ahnkutte Siwash, the oldtime Indians. "Klaska catchim boy—one boy hyiu chickamin—klaska wantum pight. Catchim hyiu boy, sometime Kimsquit, sometime any kind place. Lots man he pight. Me halo stop that time. Stlong stick makim dely piah, delate stlong, pightim. Calibou bone makim halo la hache. Nooskulies one mountain good, dely stick, stone halo kokshut, ahnkutte. Me boy that time. Plaser Lake dog muckamuck, halo sapolill, halo shugah. Me papa Nautley Siwash, Leon, Tcheslatta Siwash me. Me mama he papa Quesnel Siwash. Me mama he bludah hyas tyee. He come Ulkatcho catchim klootchman. One whiteman Kluskus he stop, Siwash he tellim stoly."

For the benefit of Ruth and me, the trader said, "Sundayman's story goes something like this. In the old days, Indians captured boys to trade—they were worth a lot of money—sometimes from Kimsquit, sometimes other places. It caused big fights. Sundayman was a boy at the time and he ran away. Caribou antler was no match for steel axe. His father was a Nautley Indian. In those days at Fraser Lake they ate dog meat, no bread, no sugar. He was born at Cheslatta. His mother's father was a Quesnel Indian. His mother's brother was a big chief. He came to Ulkatcho for a wife. The Indians told this to a white man at Kluskus."

Stillas had more recent events on his mind. He said, "Squinas Louis yahka tikegh skin catchim nika tlapline. Nika wawa tyee kopa tlapline. Me tlapline beaver stop. All time catchim me tlapline. Dat man stealim—mo bettah yaka stop kopa papa Nacoontloon. Ulkatcho all time hyiu hunt, byemby halo muckamuck. Some man halo soonyia. Too much Ulkatcho man hunt. Mo bettah he catchim cattle."

John Ward interpreted. "Stillas says that Louis Squinas wants to trap on his trapline. Stillas told the boss of traplines about it. Stillas has beaver on his trapline. Louis traps them all the time. He steals—it would be better if he stayed with his father at Anahim Lake. Ulkatcho people hunt too much; by and by there will be no food. Some of them have no cattle. They hunt too much. It would be better if they went in for cattle."

The three old men rose. "Goodbye," they said together and left.

"Well!" exclaimed the trader, looking at Ruth. "This is a special occasion. You are the first white woman to enter my store."

"I am surprised to find a store at Ulkatcho at all," said Ruth.

"It is a small business, to be sure. I am here only a few months a year, mostly in the winter during trapping season. The Indians themselves are away much of the year, catching and drying fish, hunting, digging potatoes for Norwegian farmers in Bella Coola, haying for ranchers at Anahim Lake, visiting relatives at Ootsa Lake or the Blackwater. They are on the move all the time, even in winter. There are only a hundred or so Ulkatcho Stick Indians, and not all of them live here, like Captain Harry at Qualcho Lake and Kwahoose at Salmon River. Old Capoose lived at Abuntlet Lake until he died a few years ago. He had the fur trade business in Ulkatcho pretty well tied up. Paul Krestinuk, my partner, expanded his business to Ulkatcho after Capoose was gone. With stores at Nazko, Kluskus and Ulkatcho, we scratch out a living."

"One of the nurses wondered why anyone would want to live at Ulkatcho," said Ruth. "It seems so desolate."

"The country supports these people well. There are plenty of fish in the lakes and rivers, caribou and marmots in the mountains, and recently, lots of moose. The forests are full of furbearing animals. There are enough wild meadows for a few horses but not enough for ranching. So the country does not attract white people—except for a solitary fur trader, a Catholic priest once a year, if that, and the occasional doctor. It is still Indian country."

"I've heard about priest time," I said. "What is it?"

"It is a week in early June when the Catholic priest comes to Ulkatcho. The priest is Father Thomas, an Oblate of Mary Immac-

Lassis West, Amie Leon, Dorothy Leon and Joseph Johnny at Ulkatcho.

ulate, a Frenchman, the only priest these Indians have seen." The trader reflected a moment. "That may not be strictly true. Charlie West told me that when he was a boy Father Morice came to Ulkatcho once. Charlie said Father Morice showed the Indians the Catholic business but never returned. Father Thomas has been coming here for thirty-five years. The Indians don't know what to make of him—an old man in a dress—but they leave their camps at priest time to come to Ulkatcho to learn more about the Catholic business."

"That doesn't make sense," I said.

"The Indians love a celebration," John Ward explained. "The priest does all the marrying all at once in June. And after he leaves, the Ulkatchos have a great time racing horses and playing lahal. They might even have a small potlatch, which is immoral in the eyes of the church and illegal in the eyes of the government."

"What is potlatch? What is lahal?" I asked. Ulkatcho was more interesting than the sagging log cabins and sombre forest suggested.

"A potlatch is an Indian celebration where people get together, eat a lot and give things away."

"That's against the law?" Ruth was astounded. "It sounds like Christmas!"

"The Indians think so too. On the coast where they have gone to jail for potlatching, they have big weddings at Christmas time. Potlatch gifts are wrapped in Christmas paper and wedding paper to deceive the Indian agent and the police."

"And lahal?" I reminded the trader.

"Lahal is a guessing game where bets are placed. The players sit opposite each other on the ground. One player has a small stick or bone which he moves rapidly from hand to hand. The whole time there is loud drumming and chanting—it is quite hypnotizing. The drumming stops suddenly and the opposing player guesses which hand the stick is in. If he guesses correctly he wins the amount gambled. Usually only men play lahal, but there is a story of a woman who became wealthy at the game. She would sit opposite her male opponent with her legs spread. Carrier Indians are generally modest

113

and ashamed of indecent exposure. The woman's behaviour took the edge off the men's concentration."

"We looked into the church," said Ruth. "We were surprised that the Catholic Church would spend money on a big church at little Ulkatcho."

"The Catholic Church does not spend money on Ulkatcho," replied the trader. "The Indians whipsawed the lumber for the church building and they built it. The priest bought the religious furnishings with money collected from fines he levied on the Indians for their sins. The Indians also provide food and accommodation for Father Thomas on his circuit and they supply the horses."

"That is unjust," I said.

"Souls are saved," the trader pointed out with a smile. "That is no small thing for a believer. The Indians went along with the Catholic business willingly. The priest organized them into a kind of church government. He chose a church chief, a captain, a watchman, a song leader and a bell ringer. Some Indians took on names like Chantyman which means song man—the priest is French— and Sundayman."

"Now I understand why there are Stick Indian captains so far from the ocean," I exclaimed. "They are church captains."

We had let our horses graze unfettered: a mistake. In the morning John Ward came down to our camp to let us know that an Indian had seen them at the second meadow west of Ulkatcho. Ingraham volunteered to retrieve them. A sixteen-mile ride would give him a break from Ulkatcho, a place with few attractions for a boy.

Ingraham returned with our horses and a band of Indians. They were handsome people who favoured brightly coloured clothing, particularly startling silk neckerchiefs. They gave colour and liveliness to the sober country.

"A gala afternoon for the white medicine man at Ulkatcho," I said lightly.

Dr. McLean took offence. "There is an infinite difference between a heathen medicine man and a doctor," he retorted. "It is the difference between ignorance and enlightenment, between falsehood and truth."

I had not expected the outburst. I turned to John Ward who had come down to observe the activity. "What do you think is the difference, John?"

The trader took the chance of getting involved in somebody else's wrangle. "The Indians go to the medicine man when they are sick because he is the only healer they have most of the time. Father Thomas comes through the country once a year with bottles of bear grease and snake oil—I am not joking—and the Indians try his remedies. Now you missionary doctors arrive with medicine and shiny instruments. How are the Indians to judge? They try you all. Each time, some people get better and some don't. The medicine man charges ten dollars or something worth ten dollars. He returns his fee if the patient does not recover. He does his best."

Dr. McLean began examining the group of prospective patients who had just arrived. The black, sparkling eyes indicated no diseases, and the doctor found none, except for decayed teeth. He used gas to anaesthetize two children for difficult tooth extractions. Fear darkened the faces of the parents when the children lost consciousness. There were surprised cries of relief when the children came to life again.

John Ward explained what probably was going on in the minds of the Indians when the general anaesthetic took effect. "The Indians believe they have a soul which is visible only to a shaman. A person becomes unconscious when the soul leaves the body. Only a medicine man can see the soul and return it to the body."

Our horses wandered off in the evening. We recovered Dream, Peanuts and Dan, and tethered them. By morning the rest of the bunch, except for Molly, had returned.

Ruth and I stayed behind to search for the missing horse. The others headed south to the Cahoose place called Salmon River (the old name for the Dean River). Ivy Whitmore was prepared to walk since Molly was her mount. But Ingraham loaned her Pinto. He could aim his slingshot better on foot.

Molly's tracks led up the hill toward Ulkatcho village. We searched the hillside thoroughly and found nothing. At noon, discouraged, we rode over to John Ward's store. I enjoyed Ward's easy conversation and knowledge of the country. It was a relief from Dr. McLean's brusqueness and obsession with hunting and religion. Ward had the down-to-earth outlook of a trader. Catholic priests and missionary doctors suffering in the wilderness for abstract principles puzzled him. "Even the Good Samaritan did not ride about the country looking for people to help," he declared. "He only helped people he met while going about his business."

A few Indians entered the store silently in moccasined feet. Trade was done through credit, which they referred to as "jawbone." Accounts would be settled with furs in the winter.

We returned to our deserted campsite at Gatcho Lake, hoping Molly had come back to look for the other horses. Indeed she had. We put her saddle on her and headed south ten miles to the Cahoose place.

The others had set up camp on a grassy slope at the edge of the Dean River. Rainbow trout jumped in the lazy current. Ingraham was tossing a hook out and pulling them in, one every cast. Beyond the river, the Rainbow Mountains rose gently into the western sky.

I pulled the saddles off Dream, Peanuts and Molly. They moved off toward the rest of the bunch on the meadow east of camp. At the edge of the meadow on a rise of land sat the log cabins of the Cahoose family. Old Kwahoose had chosen a magnificent family seat.

At supper Dr. McLean said, "The Indians tell me that some of the people who want to see us won't be here for several days. I have arranged with Tommy Cahoose to guide us into the Rainbows. Tommy says there are lots of moose."

I was elated. There was nothing I wanted more than to get to the renowned mountains that bleed. I did not point out that the next day was August 28. Moose hunting season was due to open on September 1. Our trip to the mountains and hunting season would not overlap.

We had our horses packed by eight-thirty, the time Tommy

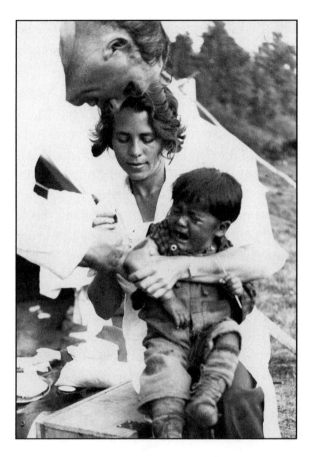

Dr. Herman McLean and Ivy Whitmore inject pertussis (whooping cough) serum into an Ulkatcho Indian boy.

Cahoose was scheduled to appear. At ten o'clock we started for the Dean River ford without him. He appeared shortly and guided us across the river to an obscure hunting trail leading southwest through meadows and burnt timber.

Tommy Cahoose did not chop downed trees from the trail; instead he jumped his horse over them. This method of travel was exceedingly trying. Eventually Dr. McLean and I took turns chopping the trail clear. While I waited my turn I had to smile at the tableau before me: the medical superintendent of the Bella Coola General Hospital, bathed in sweat, attacking fire-killed jackpine, while his Indian guide resplendent in embroidered moosehide jacket and cowboy hat sat on his horse supervising.

The forest thinned into clumps. We followed linked openings,

117

no longer trying to hold to the indistinct trail.

At the timberline we camped. Ingraham went back down to the forest for tent poles and dry wood.

The interior plateau spread below us, disappearing in blue haze in the distance, except for the Ilgachuz Mountains just across the Dean River and the solitary loaf of Anahim Peak nearby, a strange outlier of the Rainbows and the principal landmark of the country.

After supper the doctor and Tommy rode off. Shortly we heard the report of a rifle, then another.

At dusk the doctor and the Indian walked into camp.

"Well, blow me down and call me Shorty," I exclaimed. "A couple of pedestrians. Did you shoot your horses? We heard two shots."

Tommy Cahoose looked sheepish.

Dr. McLean replied triumphantly, "I shot a moose, a bull as big as a horse. He went down on my second shot."

"Congratulations," I said. "I still don't understand why you are afoot. Did you leave your horses to guard the carcass?"

The doctor explained, "We dismounted when we spotted the moose. There were no trees or bushes nearby, so we ground-tied our horses and crawled ahead for a shot. It was a good shot, too, but it made the horses bolt. Tommy went after the horses while I dressed the moose. He couldn't find them. We had to start back to camp while there was still enough light to see our way."

"You have two more horses to pray for," I said, immediately wishing I hadn't. I tried to cover the remark with, "We shall eat well at this camp. Out-of-season moose has the best flavour." The devil was in me.

The doctor did not try to defend himself. He had yielded to temptation. He was filled with guilt and remorse. He declared, "I have sinned by shooting a moose out of season. In James, God says, 'For whosoever shall keep the whole law, and yet offend in one point, he is guilty of all.' The Lord has punished me by taking my horse."

Ruth muttered, "James again."

I looked at the Stick Indian. "What do you think, Tommy?"

"I think I catch that horse."

The doctor asked us to join him at the campfire for a prayer of contrition. "O God, who is in every circumstance of life, I thank you for showing your presence tonight. I acknowledge the wrong I have done. Through it, in your wisdom, you have provided a lesson to us. We must obey the laws of those whom you have put in authority over us. I beseech you, God, to forgive my sin, for I am truly repentant. Amen."

There was a long silence. Finally, Ingraham, a country boy for whom hunting laws were not the word of God, said, "I figure you haven't done anything very wrong shooting a moose a few days ahead of season. What is the difference, a day here or there, in the Rainbow Mountains?"

Tommy Cahoose agreed. "God too tough on you. He take horse, saddle, bridle; cost maybe hundred dollar. Just for one God damn moose. Lotsa moose this place."

Ingraham seemed to accept Dr. McLean's belief in a personal God; he put it forward in a practical way. "Why don't you make a deal with God? Tell him you will give the moose to the starving Indians if he will give you your horse back."

There was another long silence. Then we went to bed.

In our tent I whispered to Ruth, "Ingraham had a good idea, except that the Indians aren't starving."

In the night I awoke to the sound of something approaching camp. I heard the clunk of a horseshoe on rock. I pushed aside the tent flap to investigate. In the light of a gibbous moon I saw two saddled horses with reins dangling. I went out, tied them to trees and unsaddled them.

I was awakened a second time by a shout at dawn. "Hallelujah! The Lord has forgiven me! He has returned my horse!"

The doctor was standing in front of his tent in his underwear.

Prayers of thanks were offered at breakfast for both the hotcakes and the strayed horses.

Tommy Cahoose and I went to fetch the rest of the horses. As we rode out, Tommy remarked, "That doctin man, he want to go to

Dorothy Sill, Teddy
Cahoose, Mary Sill
at Ulkatcho.

heaven awful bad. Prays every day. Some day two time twice."

We packed up and set out for the dead moose. Dr. McLean had given it to Tommy. The two men butchered it, then covered it with brush. We took ten pounds of tenderloin and continued our sightseeing trip.

We rode across the eastern slope of Tsitsutl Peak, the highest volcano in the Rainbow Range. Tsitsutl means painted mountain in the Carrier Indian language; the rocks and flowers on the broad, terraced slope justified it.

Tommy Cahoose told us that in the old days the Ulkatcho people collected volcanic glass near Anahim Peak for knives and spears. I asked him if people had lived in the mountains. The question seemed absurd to him. "No God damn fish stop this place," he said. Who would want to live in a place without fish?

120

Tommy guided us down a steep lava flow onto a broad plateau. Then he turned about without a farewell. We saw him next as a silhouette on the ridge behind us.

Below us on the flat, forested country northeast of the Dean River, white plumes of smoke rose like giant mushrooms, betraying nascent forest fires. To the northwest, the Coast Mountains stood out sharply on the skyline, grey-blue and white; they were jagged granite mountains unlike the rounded volcanic ones we travelled in. We felt a tremendous sense of freedom, enhanced by the desertion of our guide who had no confidence in us. "You get lost," he had said.

We continued across the broad skirts of Tsitsutl Peak, moving past shallow lakes fed by small glaciers, crunching over lava shingles that broke under the horses' hooves, scaring up ptarmigan which fled with mechanical chuckles, and perplexing curious caribou.

The gentle slope ended abruptly. We bunched up and looked into Paradise Valley. Beef Trail Creek glimmered between the trees at the bottom. The hillside was too steep and forested for our horses. We turned east, descending to the edge of the forest where we could find firewood and tent poles.

In the morning the sky was overcast, the underside of the clouds mauve. Forest fire smoke spread over the whole country.

At breakfast Dr. McLean asserted, "I am able to forecast the weather today through scripture." He quoted from memory, "'When it is evening, ye say, It will be fair weather: for the sky is red. And in the morning, It will be foul weather today: for the sky is red and lowring.' The gospel according to Saint Matthew, Chapter Sixteen."

Nobody responded. We could sense the approach of rain. We did not need confirmation from scripture.

Finally I said, "The nurses have already diagnosed pediculous weather. You medical people are more full of information than Eaton's catalogue."

We rode north over open alpine country into slanting rain. The colourful slopes of the previous day had become drab. Forest fire smoke filled the valleys, and mountains rose above the smoke like islands. We were horseback mariners cruising a sea of smoke.

I stopped at the bottom of the canyon where Tommy Cahoose had left us. "I'll go ahead to check the remains of the moose," I said. "If a grizzly bear has found the gut pile, he may dispute ownership."

I led Dream out of the canyon, then rode across the flat country to the moose remains. The meat was gone. Tommy Cahoose had come back with packhorses the same day he left us.

I signalled from the top of the canyon for the others to come up. I had no idea where the trail entered the forest from the tundra—all the patches of alpine fir looked the same—but when I gave Dream her head, without even slowing down she found horse tracks leading into the bush.

We reached the Cahoose place at three o'clock, very tired and wet. We erected our three tents near the Dean River again and turned our horses loose on good grass. Our Indian patients had arrived and were camped nearby.

In the morning Ruth felt ill. Ingraham made flapjacks using the bannock recipe but with sloppy dough.

I asked Dr. McLean about Ruth.

"Have you heard of morning sickness?" he asked rhetorically.

"I am only twenty-three." I tried to joke to cover my feelings.

An Indian rode into camp. He looked at Dr. McLean and said, "Tenas memaloose. Baby die."

The doctor and Mary Munn rode over to the Indian camp on Dan and Pinto. They returned presently, not with a dead child but with a living three-year-old boy.

The boy coughed violently. Mary Munn wrapped him in blankets under a tent fly. "This is Mike," she said when I approached with my camera. "He has whooping cough. He was sitting on a log at the Indian camp. He was so sick he was nearly falling over. His parents don't know what to do with him."

Dr. McLean added, "We shall care for him here until we leave. I shall try to persuade his parents to let us take him to Bella Coola for hospitalization."

The doctor and Ivy Whitmore returned to the Indian camp with pertussis antibacterial serum to inoculate the other children against whooping cough.

At our camp Ruth made baking powder biscuits and soup. Mary Munn offered some to Mike. He ate a little. From time to time he burst into terrible fits of coughing ending in a dramatic intake of air, a whoop which nearly tore his body apart.

After lunch I went up to the Cahoose cabins where the doctor and nurse were doing medical examinations. There I met Prong, Plank, Frank and Gus Cahoose. He was sitting on a blanket on the porch of a log cabin, a single person with many monikers. The doctor had just examined him.

"Prong was in the Bella Coola Hospital for a year," Dr. McLean told me. "He has tuberculosis of the bone. Tuberculosis of the bone

Gus Cahoose, ill with tuberculosis, at Salmon River.

A horse loaded with whipsawed boards and a coffin containing a child's body at Salmon River.

has less effect upon general health than pulmonary tuberculosis does, and Prong's condition did not change. When Indian Affairs ordered that chronic cases be sent home, I had to discharge Prong. He was weak after a year in a hospital bed. His relatives lifted him onto his horse, but he could ride only an hour at a time, followed by a couple of hours' rest. It must have taken them weeks to ride from Bella Coola to Salmon River. I did not expect to see him again alive. But here he is, cheerful and certain that he is getting better."

When the doctor left, I stayed to talk to the optimistic young Indian. I had empathy with someone crippled and determined to overcome the disability.

"I want to tell you something, Prong," I started.

"My name not Plong, it Plank," he said, struggling with the word.

I puzzled a moment, then perceived what was going on. Stick

Indians could not pronounce F or R.

"Ah, your name is Frank," I beamed, wondering whether naming a Stick Indian Frank was somebody's idea of a joke.

"Plank Cahoose," he affirmed. "Andy Chlistensen call me Gus."

"You have more names than you need," I said. "I just want to tell you that a few years ago I could not walk. Now I walk and ride horses. Maybe someday you will walk and ride too."

"Someday," he agreed.

"Good luck, Gus," I said to Frank.

Gus Cahoose was riding horses a year later and subsequently was a big game guide for many years in the West Chilcotin country.

In the evening, Joe Cahoose rode into our camp leading the packhorse we had lost at Slough Grass Meadow on our third day out. Joe had found the animal at a hay camp west of Ulkatcho. This, our thirteenth horse, had been travelling behind us for thirteen days, picking out our tracks and scent from among the Indians' horses. He was fat, though fly-bitten. I intended to put the shirker to a final week of hard work. He would carry a heavy pack to relieve the sore-backed horses who had been carrying his load for two weeks.

Dr. McLean gave Joe Cahoose a dollar. Then he turned to me. He said, "Now do you believe in the power of prayer? You have just seen a demonstration of the unchanging trustworthiness of God."

Uncertain of what to believe, I shot back, "I wish God had come up with a demonstration that did not involve taking a packhorse. I had to overload the other horses because of it. How am I to excuse the sore backs to Tommy Walker? If they are a result of God's little tricks, you explain them to Tommy Walker. That's your line of business, not mine!"

"You do not understand," the doctor said calmly. "God returned the horse; he did not take it."

"Who took it, then?"

"The imperfection of the world."

September 2 was Sunday. I was the first one up at nine o'clock. Ruth followed shortly. We made breakfast for ourselves and then walked up to the Cahoose cabins with a camera.

The Indians were preparing for the burial of a child that had died two days earlier. The coffin was made of boards split from a log. It was covered with black sateen. On the lid was a cross of yellow silk. Two cushions made of orange cloth stuffed with grass were inside.

Old Kwahoose held a string of beads. He and his wife said a brief prayer in Chinook. The small body was placed in the box on the cushions.

A fat black horse was packed with a load of short pieces of whipsawn lumber, perhaps for a rough box. The top pack was the coffin wrapped in canvas sitting on sacks of hay. Two young men set out for the cemetery at Ulkatcho on horseback leading the packhorse. Others followed at intervals.

Dr. McLean came to the Cahoose cabins in an attempt to persuade Mike's parents to let us take the boy with whooping cough to the hospital in Bella Coola. He cajoled in English and Chinook. He pointed out that it would cost the parents nothing. He warned that the boy would probably die without hospital care. The parents were obdurate.

At our camp the nurses fed Mike supper and prepared him for his return home. He was a gaunt picture of misery. He twitched spasmodically. Dr. McLean said that the twitching indicated approaching death.

The doctor decided to take the boy to his parents on the horse that Joe Cahoose had returned. The horse was skittish. It jumped away from the saddle and faced the doctor defiantly. In a fit of temper, the doctor tied the horse to a tree, pulled a lash rope from the equipment pile and whipped the animal viciously. "You evil brute! I will show you who is in control!" he bellowed. He strode to his tent.

Almost immediately Ingraham emerged from the same tent, walked to the horse, saddled it and rode away. He returned with Tommy Cahoose to pick up Mike.

Tommy approached me first. He said, "You pay horse feed. He eat lotsa God damn grass."

"What!" I shot back. "We came all the way from Bella Coola to give your people free medical attention. We paid you to guide us into the Rainbow Mountains. We chopped out your hunting trail. We gave you a whole moose. Now you want to be paid for the grass our horses eat. Talk to Dr. McLean!" I pointed to the tent.

Tommy Cahoose went to the tent. The doctor came out. The two men went over to the equipment pile. Dr. McLean handed a packsaddle to the Indian. My heart dropped. We would be short a packhorse still.

With the child Mike in one arm and the packsaddle resting on the pommel, Tommy Cahoose walked his horse slowly back to the Cahoose cabins.

In the morning, while we were packing, an attractive young Indian woman trotted a good horse into camp.

"Somebody doctin this place?" she asked.

"I am the doctor," said Dr. McLean. "Do you need help?"

"Tooth hurt bad," the woman said.

She swung from the saddle, went up to Dr. McLean and opened her mouth. He looked in.

"I will pull it," he said.

He took forceps from the hospital box and pulled. The tooth came free, gleaming white, red and grey at the end of the forceps. No matter how often observed, it was a moment charged with triumph.

"What is your name?"

"Josephine Capoose. Antoine Capoose, he my daddy."

"Do you want your tooth, Josephine?"

She shook her head. "I don't like that one."

She spat blood, swung into the saddle, nodded thanks to the doctor and urged her horse into a lope, heading for Ulkatcho.

"What a striking figure!" exclaimed Ivy Whitmore. "If I had met her before I knew what a hard life these Stick Indians have, I would envy her."

I was seething as we continued packing. We were short a packsaddle now that we had enough packhorses. Finally my feelings broke loose. I demanded of the doctor, "Why did you give Tommy Cahoose a packsaddle?"

"It was payment for pasturage."

"Haven't we given the Indians more than enough to make up for it?"

"That's not the way they see it."

"Do you?"

"We are on a mission of mercy. The people we serve should not be incommoded by us. We serve God through them."

We got away about ten o'clock. The doctor rode far ahead; he was out of sight most of the day. Ruth felt ill and fell far behind.

We rode south across broad, hummocky meadows and through monotonous forests of small, uniform pines. The country offered no site with all the essential elements for a horse camp: horse feed, clean water, firewood and space for tents. We had to push on.

For Ruth's sake I was ready to call a halt anywhere with horse feed. Abruptly the country relented. We came upon an ideal camping place on an oxbow in the Dean River. To complete our small paradise, there were no mosquitoes or blackflies.

I arose to a frosty dawn. While I lit a fire, Ingraham went to the meadow to count horses. He returned chilled to the bone but with the gratifying count of thirteen. He returned to his blankets, clothed to his hat, to await breakfast.

The long miles of swamp meadow and jackpine continued. Mary Munn and her horse provided unintentional comic relief to break the monotony. The horse, Cream, a soft three-year-old with an independent mind, lay down on the trail we were following. The nurse had to step out of the saddle.

Ruth remarked, "It looks like Cream has dissolved your partnership, Mary."

"It is your turn to carry the horse," put in Ingraham.

I added, "Without a horse you are confronted with an extended act of pedestrianism."

The end of a swung rope encouraged the horse to continue the trudge.

About noon we came to a road and a telephone line strung on jackpine poles. As Mary Munn rode under the line, it brushed her hat onto the road. On dismounting, she released the halter rope of the packhorse she was leading, and the horse walked off. She retrieved the packhorse, but her saddlehorse drifted away. No sooner had she caught her saddlehorse than the wind blew off her broad-brimmed hat. The flying hat spooked the horses, and they both broke loose. The nurse stood in the middle of the road hatless, horseless and near tears.

Soon after we got Mary Munn remounted, we came to the Capoose ranch on the east side of Abuntlet Lake. It had a prosperous air. The log buildings and corrals were well built. The haying crew at the ranch told us that Old Capoose, the Stick Indian trader who had built the ranch, had died two or three years earlier. The outfit was run by his daughters Josephine and Doll, and Doll's husband, Clayton Mack, a Bella Coola Indian.

I asked the haying crew if they were worried about the forest fire burning just east of the ranch. Not at all, they said; the wind was from the west.

The country opened up suddenly, becoming more meadow than forest. For the first time we experienced the expanse of the plateau we had moved onto. I felt as though I were back on the prairies. We crossed one big meadow after another and encountered herds of Hereford range cattle.

We camped beside cold, clear Christensen Creek which flowed from the Ilgachuz Range, the best water we had tasted in weeks. Dr. McLean crossed the creek to visit Andy and Dorothy Christensen who had recently moved to Anahim Lake from Bella Coola to build the biggest ranch in the Anahim Lake country.

Dr. McLean returned with five loaves of bread and a bucket of milk. He told us that the Christensens were out of meat (ranchers did not eat their own beef) and that he might go hunting with an Indian called Casimiel (baptised Casimir by Father Thomas). The rest of us were delighted with the prospect of a day of relaxation in this marvellous bowl of high prairie.

The doctor prayed through the night. In the morning he said that he was not going hunting. The moral problem he faced was that hunting moose meat for Christensen's haying crew was not God's work; it neither healed the sick, comforted the afflicted nor witnessed to the unsaved.

When Casimiel rode into camp with his rifle, Dr. McLean immediately changed his mind. He rushed about preparing a lunch, putting on his puttees and checking his rifle. In a few minutes the two hunters rode out. A contented silence fell on our camp.

Ruth and I went over to meet Dorothy and Andy Christensen. Bob Bowser, the Hudson's Bay Company storekeeper from Anahim Lake, was visiting. We accompanied him to Clesspocket Meadow where we delivered lunch to the haying crew. The men were constructing great volcanoes of hay using ropes and pulleys on A-frames.

Dr. McLean arrived back in camp late in the afternoon exceedingly weary and dispirited. He and Casimiel had ridden for miles—the doctor estimated thirty miles—along the edge of the forest fire, expecting fleeing animals. They saw nothing. The two men were dirty and smoky, and the doctor had burned his puttees.

After supper Casimiel returned with his wife. Dr. McLean pulled two of her teeth. Those two rotten teeth salvaged the doctor's day; they assuaged his feelings of guilt. Casimiel invited us to a poker game with the haying crew. He reported that one man had won more than five dollars the previous night. The doctor declined the invitation for all of us, adding, "Sufficient unto the day is the evil thereof. Matthew six, thirty-four." Casimiel and his wife rode off. The sun sank like a ball of blood through the forest fire smoke which filled the Dean River Valley.

In the morning Dr. McLean rode back to the Capoose ranch for a signature he needed on a legal form. The rest of us were invited for coffee at the Christensen cabin while we waited. Andy Christensen entertained us with a story about his neighbour, Clayton Mack, who had had to marry Antoine Capoose's daughter twice.

Building a
haystack at
Clesspocket
Ranch near
Anahim
Lake.

Andy said, "Clayton and Doll were married the first time by the United Church preacher in Bella Coola where Clayton grew up, even though they lived at Capoose's place at Abuntlet Lake. The United Church preacher was available all the time, but the Catholic priest came through the country only once a year, if that. When Father Thomas arrived here at priest time and discovered that Doll Capoose, one of his parishioners, had gone through a form of marriage in a Protestant church, he was furious. In his eyes that was no marriage at all; the young woman was living in sin. Besides, it looked like the United Church was sheep rustling from the Catholic Church. The priest confronted Clayton and fined him ten dollars. Clayton did not have ten dollars but he went through a Catholic wedding to set

131

things straight. I don't know whether he ever paid the fine."

On our way to Anahim Lake we followed a rutted wagon road across meadows and through Bryant's homestead. Shortly we came to a road with a set of automobile tracks. We followed the tracks to Anahim Lake, a settlement consisting of the old Squinas house and a new Hudson's Bay Company store.

The Indians at the Squinas house were the last prospective patients for our medical mission. They were in good health. We completed our visit with the purchase of moosehide gloves from a cheerful Indian woman who smoked fat rollings.

An early start in the morning was denied us by Mose and Bluey, two of Tommy Walker's horses. During the night they had started east toward Towdystan, their previous home. Their tracks were easy to follow on the dirt road, and Ingraham and I soon overtook them. But dreams of reaching the Precipice that day were dashed.

On the trail Mose persistently tried to turn back. Ivy Whitmore, who had the responsibility for keeping Mose in line, rode off-trail time and again. She got farther and farther behind. Eventually Mose made a break and headed east at a gallop.

I gave the lead to Ingraham, telling him to go slowly. I went after the errant packhorse with Ruth. Ivy Whitmore stayed behind to look for a wrist watch she had lost. Dr. McLean helped her in the search.

Out of earshot, I scoffed to Ruth, "They don't have a chance of finding Ivy's watch in this vast wilderness."

We caught up with Mose three miles down the trail and hurried him back with a stinging rope. On the way we overtook Dr. McLean and Ivy Whitmore.

"We found my watch," declared the delighted nurse. "It was hanging on a tree branch like an ornament. I must have pushed the branch aside and the strap caught on it. It is a miracle!"

I glanced at Dr. McLean. His face was impassive.

We camped at a small meadow called Big Meadow. I picketed all the horses.

We had scarcely begun the next day's ride when we came to

the end of the interior plateau. The flat lava that lay under the Anahim Lake country ended in columnar cliffs. This place was called the Precipice. The Telegraph Trail descended in zigzags down the Precipice to luxuriant meadows. The air felt softer.

Milo and Andrew Ratcliff were racing thunderheads that were heading for their hay field. Ruth and I stayed to help the haymakers at the Precipice while the rest of our outfit went down the Telegraph Trail to Atnarko. We outraced the rain by half an hour. Our reward was fresh vegetables direct from the garden for supper. After three weeks of camp food they were ambrosia.

Ruth and I rose early on September 9, hoping to reach our outfit before it hit the trail. We dropped quickly down the switchbacks of the Telegraph Trail under the wire of the telegraph line. The trail crossed back and forth over the Hotnarko River on log bridges. Only government trails had bridges.

The good trail, soft air and eager horses sensing journey's end made us reluctant to hurry even as we hurried.

We overtook the others at Belarko. Ingraham had assumed my place at the head of the packtrain. Our frying-pan-sized horseman was finishing his trip with honour. He had acquired a lot of savvy in three weeks; he had learned something about horses.

We climbed the sandhill above the Atnarko River and then descended under magnificent Douglas fir trees to the Stuie flats.

Dr. McLean remarked, "This trail is much pleasanter than the Canoe Crossing Trail. Ecclesiastes was correct: 'Better the end of a thing than the beginning thereof.'"

I could tell which book of the Bible the doctor was currently reading by his quotations.

We halted at the edge of the dirt road that ran in front of Tommy Walker's Stuie Lodge and began to unpack. As the sore backs came to view, Tommy Walker became histrionic. I mildly suggested that he shape his packsaddles to fit his horses' backs. He did not take the advice meekly. Instead he ascended to new heights of dramatic art. There was nothing I could do about sore backs then, just as I had been unable to throughout the trip. They needed time to heal, free of packs.

Ruth and I headed down the road on Dream and Peanuts to stay overnight at Hober's farm at Firvale, a sort of re-enactment of our arrival in Bella Coola Valley nearly a year earlier.

Before we were out of earshot we heard Dr. McLean admonish Tommy Walker with advice from Ecclesiastes: "Be not hasty in thy spirit to be angry: for anger resteth in the bosom of fools."

Cliff Kopas in his wife's pajama bottoms on the beach at Gatcho Lake.

INTERLUDE TWO

Through our first winter in the Bella Coola Valley, Ruth and I had lived in a shack on Frank and Laura Ratcliff's farm at Lower Bella Coola. Following our trip to Ulkatcho, Dr. McLean invited us to reside in the caretaker's suite in the Bella Coola Hospital. The doctor wanted a man in the building at night to feed the furnace with cordwood. Otherwise the night nurse had to do it.

One night in February, 1935, Dr. McLean and a nurse met me at the top of the hospital stairs and accompanied me along the brown-linoleumed corridor. As we approached Ruth's room the silence stabbed at me. An hour before, there had been hushed noise, activity, hope, effort. Now these were absent.

At my elbow the doctor was talking. "I would like you to know that we did everything humanly possible to save her. Please know that this is God's will."

At the closed door we stopped. The doctor put his hand on my shoulder for a brief moment. "You must be brave," he said. "The nurse will be here if you wish anything done."

Dr. McLean walked away, and the nurse opened the door for me.

The unmistakable smell of human suffering greeted my nostrils as I crossed the threshold. Ruth was lying on the bed, her hair neatly brushed on the pillow. Her eyes were closed, and her face had the appearance of sleep.

I stepped toward her, expecting, in spite of what the doctor had said, that she would open her eyes and smile at me as she had so often in the past. That neatly brushed hair—it was normal for her to have her hair beautifully brushed. All this was to be a pleasant announcement that she was getting better. I had never allowed myself to think otherwise.

But as I reached the side of the bed, I noticed a film of moisture on her brow and I saw her hands outside the bedcovers swollen as if by struggle. There was no opening of eyes, no smile. Finally it was the nurse who convinced me.

"Her passing was peaceful," she said quietly.

I knew it then. Rebellion rose in me. The crossing of the final pass in itself might have been peaceful, but the approaches to the pass had been so rough she had not lived through it. I turned in anger on the nurse, saw tears in her eyes, realized she had spoken to ease the blow to me. I turned back to the silent form on the bed.

"I'll wait outside," the nurse said.

A month earlier trouble had sent its warning, a puffy face, when the baby was expected in a few weeks. The doctor was called. Ruth was rushed upstairs to the hospital ward. Malfunctioning kidneys, the doctor had said. If labour did not commence naturally, he would have to induce it.

Ruth got worse. Her sister Violet Cole came out from Calgary. Dr. Darby from eighty-mile-distant Bella Bella arrived. Ruth was delivered of her baby son.

"We'll call him Peard Keith," Ruth said as she smiled wanly at the little bundle.

But trouble had not departed. Eclampsia developed and terrible seizures almost tore her apart.

A half hour earlier when I had visited her the doctor would allow only a brief visit. Now I could have as much time as I wanted.

The laugh that could turn a comfortless camp into a vibrant home would never ring out again. No longer would there be cheery encouragement when things were going badly. Suddenly there were no dreams.

A memory of the Goat River Trail came to my mind. Beside the trail lay a dead wolf. Someone had shot it. As we sat our horses and

Ruth Kopas with Peanuts at Bella Coola.

looked down at it, the lonely, mournful cry of its mate had echoed through the forest. "Poor thing," Ruth had sympathized, "now it will have to build its life all over again."

Ruth had never admitted death as final. "We live on in another form, maybe in another place."

I turned and left the room. The nurse looked at me questioningly. I shook my head and walked down the corridor.

The sound of a baby crying drew my attention. I saw Violet sitting in an alcove gently rocking Ruth's infant son. She was grieving, too, for her sister. Ruth would live on in her baby. As she had said, she would live on in another form.

Violet and Peard Cole in Calgary immediately adopted baby Peard Keith. I did not get to know Ruth's child.

Dr. Herman McLean left the United Church and Bella Coola in

137

1936 to become physician to the evangelical Shantymen's Christian Association on the west coast of Vancouver Island.

I stayed at Bella Coola, earning a small income from photographs and magazine articles about the area.

ACROSS THE CHILCOTIN
AT FORTY BELOW

"He doth nothing
but talk of his horse."
William Shakespeare,
*The Merchant
of Venice*

George Turner's granddaughter, Klinaklini River, January 1937.

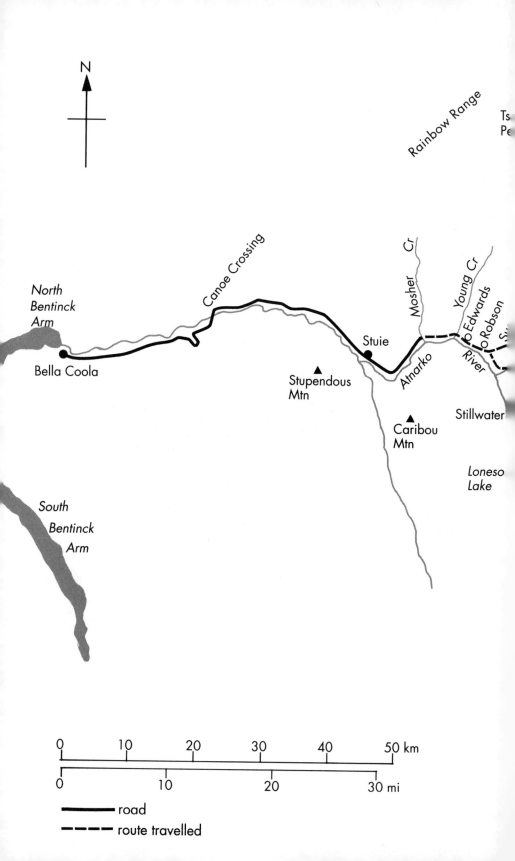

ACROSS THE CHILCOTIN 1937

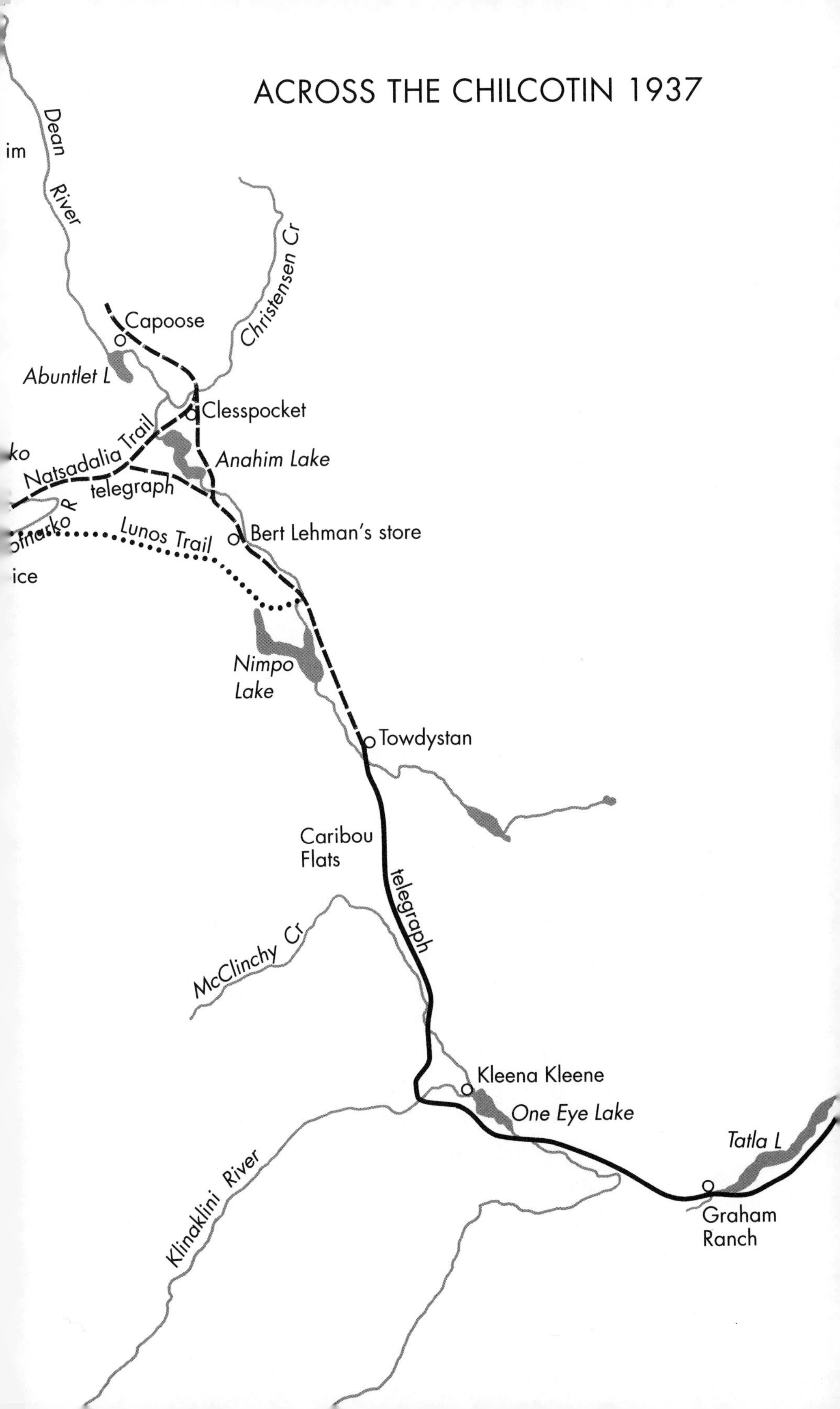

im

Dean River

Christensen Cr

Capoose

Abuntlet L

Natsadalia Trail

Clesspocket

Anahim Lake

ko

telegraph

otnarko R

ice

Lunos Trail

Bert Lehman's store

Nimpo Lake

Towdystan

Caribou Flats

McClinchy Cr

telegraph

Kleena Kleene

One Eye Lake

Tatla L

Klinaklini River

Graham Ranch

CLAYTON MACK CAME DOWN FROM HIS RANCH at Abuntlet Lake in the Anahim Lake country and told me that somebody was hunting wild horses with my horse Peanuts. "Maybe they kill that horse," he warned. "Run him too hard in cold weather."

Clayton was going back on top in January. I could go with him if I wanted. It would be wise for us to travel together. Stark cold weather and icy trails did not forgive the mistakes, miscalculations or bad luck of solitary travellers.

I felt privileged to travel with Clayton. He knew how to handle horses and in camp he was a marvellous storyteller. He liked to ride cayuses that started the day by trying to throw him. Although a Bella Coola Indian, he had adopted the horseback life of the Ulkatchos and had married one of Antoine Capoose's daughters. Doll had died of tuberculosis in the Bella Coola Hospital eighteen months earlier. Clayton and I were the same age and both young widowers.

We started out on January 9, 1937. I rode Dream, the big trail-wise buckskin mare who had come with me from Alberta in 1933. I led Popeye, a little mare packhorse purchased for the trip. She was blind in the left eye but as gentle as a moonbeam. When the Indian Agent heard that I was taking a packhorse, he persuaded me to deliver two one-gallon glass jars of cod liver oil to the Indian Health Nurse at Anahim Lake.

Clayton rode a cayuse. He did not lead a packhorse; he saw no need for one on a sixty-mile ride between Stuie and Abuntlet Lake with stopping places along the way.

We sharp-shod our horses, that is, we fitted them with calked horseshoes. Some of the calks were welded, others screwed in. We were two horseshoes short of either type. Consequently our saddlehorses were sharp-shod all round, but the packhorse only on her front feet. Horseshoes are bothersome at best; in damp snow they cause the snow to ball up under the horses' feet. But on icy trails they are essential.

The winter trail to the interior left the automobile road an hour's ride east of Stuie. Horses carrying goods to Andy Christensen's store at Anahim Lake had stepped in each other's tracks as grizzly bears do, creating a foot-hole trail in the deep snow. The only other likely travellers were the mailman—once every two weeks— and the telegraph lineman. The trail was quite beautiful: it was lined on the river side with birch trees bent in graceful arches under loads of snow and on the mountain side by cathedral-like Douglas firs.

The temperature dropped as we rode toward Atnarko. Cold air slipped over the edge of the plateau above us and flowed into the valley. A rising wind dislodged snow from the trees. Gradually we and our horses became white shadows moving slowly up the foot-hole trail under the dark forest.

A rifle shot broke the silence. Clayton, in the lead, stopped. Ahead of him stood a horse whiter than our own. In front of it, dark on the snow, a deer lay staining the snow red. Beside the deer stood a thin-faced man with a rifle.

"Where did you boys come from?" He grinned ingratiatingly. I noticed that his teeth were not spaced for a neat job of eating corn on the cob. "You ain't the mailman and you ain't the lineman. Who the hell are ya?"

We pulled our wool caps from our heads so that we could hear better and slapped the snow from them against our chaps. The hunter peered at us.

Clayton said, "I am Clayton. That other guy Kopas. We heading to Anahim. Kopas going to look for his horse. Me, I going to my place Abuntlet Lake. Nice mowitch you get."

"Just got him. You musta heard the shot."

"Thought you was shooting at us."

"I always know what I am shooting at," said the man, sounding offended. He bent to his job. "Gotta dress out this deer. Where you boys spending the night?"

"Edwards'," I said as I rode past, glad to get a word in. The man in the lead corners all the talk at trail meetings.

"Who was that?" I shouted ahead to Clayton.

He turned in his saddle and lifted an earflap on his wool cap. "What you say? Come up in lead. My horse need a spell

Earle Edwards and Cliff Kopas with Popeye and Dream at Atnarko.

from breaking trail."

I worked Dream through the snow past Popeye and Clayton's horse.

I repeated, "Who was that back there?"

"He B.C. Wright. Come from the States. He own some land up trail a bit. Never hunt on it himself—he always go somewhere else to hunt. Hard winter like this he feed lotsa deer. Always some deer on his clearing. One winter he count eighty. Nobody hunt his place. Game reserve, like. Funny bugger. I see him one time, but he don't remember me, I guess."

We came out of a cathedral of tall Douglas fir trees into a clearing. The snow deepened. Each horse stepped precisely into the hoofprints of the one ahead. On the uphill side the clearing contained a cabin and a few fruit trees, probably apple. Below the cabin a meadow held half a dozen mule deer, muzzles in the snow. A magnificent buck looked up to watch us pass.

"Old B.C., he can kill mowitch without stepping outside his cabin," commented Clayton. "He do it only once. After that no mowitch for long, long time."

144

"I'm getting pretty cold," I said. "How far to Edwards'?"

"Six mile. We walk a bit when we get back in timber. Snow too deep here. This foot-hole trail slow us down too much, wear us out."

We crossed the log bridge over Young Creek. In places the creek swirled around snow- turbaned boulders but for the most part it was concealed under snow-covered ice.

Late in the afternoon we reached a well-built cabin of hewn logs. We pulled up in front of the door.

"Hello, this place," I called.

Earle Edwards pulled the door open. He blew a plume of smoke from his pipe.

"You two look like the Royal Canadian Mounted Snowmen, but I believe I know who you are. I thought perhaps you had been delayed at Belarko by the products of Alger's still."

"We didn't stop there," I replied, too cold for a witty rejoinder. "It was the deep snow that held us up."

Earle called into the cabin. "Isabel, throw some water in the stew. Cliff and Clayton are here."

Earle tossed hay to the horses while we unpacked. We brushed ourselves free of snow and pushed into the cabin. Isabel Edwards was frying venison steaks. The coffee pot was percolating.

Maximilian Heckman, a neighbour from a homestead two miles up the trail, sat in a rustic armchair. Waving the moosehide-covered stump of his forearm, he was dramatizing a story for Ralph Edwards, Earle's brother from Lonesome Lake.

Earle introduced Ralph and Maxi to me—they already knew Clayton. The introductions were the merest break in Maxi's long and exciting yarn about his sworn enemies: wolves. Frontiersmen abhorred their way of capturing deer with their teeth.

Ralph disliked wolves, too, although his stories ran more to grizzly bears. When pressed, he and Maxi admitted that they had never heard of a wolf attacking a human. Grizzly bear attacks, on the other hand, were not uncommon.

After satisfying his need for yarning, Maxi Heckman stepped outside into a clear but moonless night. In one hand he held a bug (a tin can cut to reflect the light of a candle) and in the other he carried a rifle. He had two miles of dark trail to walk to his cabin.

"Beware of the wolves, Max," said Isabel mischievously. Maxi had spent the evening alarming the rest of us with wolf stories, but it was he who had to walk home alone in the dark.

Ralph, Clayton and I climbed a ladder to the loft above the living quarters. The warmth that rose from below soon turned our drowsiness to sleep.

We were still eating breakfast when Frank Ratcliff, Ralph's brother-in-law, arrived. He had walked down from his Stillwater cabin. His husky six-foot physique dwarfed Ralph. The two frontiersmen set off together, each with a pack on his back and a rifle under his arm, Frank striding along, Ralph doing double time on his short legs.

Clayton and I saddled our horses and packed Popeye, then swung into our saddles.

"The weather is getting colder," I observed. "Where is the sun when we need it?"

Earle Edwards said, "At this time of year the sun hides behind Caribou Mountain. It comes back in spring when the weather warms up." He turned to Clayton and said gravely, "Beware you don't frost your pedal extremities."

Clayton shot a concerned look at me. "What he mean?"

"Your feet," I said. "Don't freeze them."

Clayton grinned. "I try that one on those swamp grass ranchers at Anahim Lake. They find out I'm a smart guy when I say that." He practised the words, "Pedal extremities." He nudged his horse forward. "You bet."

We stopped at Bert Robson's homestead—the last farm in the Atnarko valley—for hay to carry with us. We knew that there was no horse feed at the Precipice, the farm in the Hotnarko valley where we would spend the night.

Bert Robson was down at the Atnarko River fishing for steelhead. His rifle, the frontiersman's constant companion, leaned against a boulder beside him.

Frank Ratcliff and Ralph Edwards at Atnarko, January 10, 1937.

"I'll have one in a few minutes," he said with assurance.

The Atnarko valley was fabulous fish and game country. It suited an outdoorsman like Bert Robson. He could fish and hunt virtually on his doorstep. Like B.C. Wright, he did not hunt on his own property. Dozens of mule deer congregated on his meadows in the winter and spring. The timber wolf, the frontiersman's competitor for game, was gunned down at every opportunity. A big one lay trussed to a sled outside Bert's cabin. A dead wolf was worth twenty-five dollars in bounty; the government did not like wolves either.

"Come inside while I clean the fish," said Bert. "Then we'll get you some hay."

Bert Robson's cabin was a veritable museum, full of memorabilia from his adventurous life. He had been born on the north coast at Port Simpson, the son of a Hudson's Bay Company trader. He learned the Tsimshian Indian language before he learned English. He went to school in Victoria and then spent four years in France through the Great War. After returning to British Columbia he worked on ships along the coast. For a time he was a purser on the Union Steamships. His shelves contained books on British Columbia history and outdoor adventure. His cabin walls were adorned with Indian baskets and whistles, mountain goat horns, German military helmets, snowshoes, caribou antlers, bayonets and daggers.

We went to the barn with four sugar sacks and pushed and stomped hay into them until they bulged like balloons. Then we slung them over our saddles behind the cantles. We were a travelling advertisement for the British Columbia Sugar Refinery.

We mounted our horses. Clayton gathered up his reins. He was about to touch a spur to his horse. He hesitated. He put both hands on his saddlehorn and leaned over his horse's withers. He looked down at Bert Robson.

"Bert," he said. "Did you ever frost your pedal extremities?"

Bert's forehead wrinkled. Then a smile played on his lips. "Clayton," he replied. "If you spend too much time talking with those Edwards brothers, nobody in this country is going to understand a thing you say."

Half an hour's ride from Bert Robson's place, we started to climb into the high country over snow-covered rockslides on a steep trail that zigzagged above Sugar Camp Creek. Far uphill, the slope slackened and the trees closed in. Birch and willow saplings bowed over the trail, weighed down by snow. Spring-loaded, they swung upward the moment they were disturbed.

Bent over our pommels, we rode beneath beautiful arches which were transformed into brief blizzards the instant our horses touched them. Snow found its way under our collars and down our backs. It landed on the cantles when we bent forward to avoid

Bert Robson with a steelhead at the Atnarko River.

A timber wolf carcass beside Bert Robson's cabin at Atnarko.

149

branches and melted when we sat back. We became wet from neck to stern.

From time to time we dismounted and walked to warm up. The effort of ploughing knee-deep between horse tracks too widely spaced for our stride made us return to the discomfort of our saddles.

Mule deer and moose had traced a maze of tracks and were still at it. We counted thirty moose. They trotted through the snow, over windfalls and across rockslides as though airborne. With the rut long over, the bulls were losing their antlers. Some had none, others had both, and a few grotesque creatures had only one. We did not count deer; they were as common as belly buttons.

Twice Clayton stopped to point out a patch of bloodstained snow and some fur. Wolves had killed two deer.

"Mowitch and moose come down from on top and stay on hillside in winter," explained Clayton. "Wolf follow them."

"The wolves are a long way from killing all the deer and moose," I observed. "But what about us? Would they attack men on horseback?"

"Never hear about it. Never happen, I guess. Lotsa story about guys scared about it. Me, I get scared sometime too. Never happen yet."

At dusk we approached a homestead under the rimrock cliff called the Precipice. A shaggy collie dog came out from the cabin yodelling strangely.

A man opened the door. "Shut up, Singer," he commanded. "Step down, boys, and come in. The dog is harmless. Ever since a horse kicked him and broke his jaw, he has been awful proud of his yodel. He does it every time he has an excuse."

"Where can we hold our horses?" I asked.

"Turn 'em loose right here. My fences are good."

We unpacked Popeye and removed the saddles and bridles from all three horses. We left the saddle blankets on the animals for warmth. Then we emptied the four gunny sacks of hay on the snow and went inside to see what sort of grub our host Jack Weldon had for us.

Clayton Mack at the bottom of the Sugar Camp Trail at Atnarko.

We ate venison steaks again and boiled spuds.

"Lots of mowitch around here this winter," remarked Jack Weldon. "Lots of moose too. No point in killing one of those big brutes. What would I do with a quarter of a ton of meat?"

"Better get some meat," advised Clayton. "We see two wolf kill on Sugar Camp Trail. Maybe no moose or mowitch sometime."

"Lots of wolves around, all right," Jack Weldon agreed. "You'll hear 'em howl tonight. The way they are knocking down the deer, they'll soon be after the moose. They don't like to tackle moose before the antlers have dropped. A moose with antlers is too dangerous for 'em. Some people say wolves are cowards. I think they are just smart."

A long moan from the ridge on the Precipice grew into a drawn-out howl. Jack Weldon's dog got to its feet, fur bristling, looked apprehensively at the door and slunk under the bed at the far side of the room.

"Singer is afraid of wolves," said Jack Weldon.

In the morning the air was clear except for floating frost

crystals. Packed snow squeaked and crunched under our feet. We loaded Popeye and were in our saddles before the pallid winter sun appeared over the ridge to the southeast. We started early because there were no stopping places between the Precipice and Anahim Lake. We had to make the journey in one day or suffer a long, cold night beside the trail with no feed for the horses.

The trail zigzagged up the face of the Precipice at first, then swung in an ascending arc around the west side, heading for the flat jackpine country of the plateau. With sharp shoes all around, the saddlehorses were surefooted. Popeye, the packhorse, had sharp shoes only on her front feet, her steering parts; on her pushers, her hind feet, she had slick steel shoes. Several times on the zigzags her hind feet slid back on a piece of ice under the snow.

At the rim of the Precipice, Clayton encountered a cornice of wind-driven snow overhanging the trail. He spurred his surefooted cayuse off the trail and around the snowdrift. Popeye tried to follow. The smooth shoes on her rear feet slipped on the frozen ground at the edge of the trail. She slid backward, vainly pawing for a grip with

Clayton Mack digging Popeye out of the snow.

her front feet. She tipped onto her side. Her feet appeared in the air from out of a mass of sliding snow. She gained momentum and disappeared in a small avalanche, then appeared again, rolled and slid head first down the long lower slope of the Precipice. She stopped sliding, and the snow which had been following her quietly covered her over. Only her tail darkened the white expanse at the bottom of the hill. Nothing moved. Popeye was buried nose first.

Clayton and I watched, immobilized by disbelief. The moment the slide stopped, Clayton leapt from his horse, threw off his chaps, and ran and slid down the hill. He dug frantically through the snow and in a moment was scooping snow from Popeye's nostrils. Then he freed her head. Her good eye was still in the snow. The mare could not move and she could not see. But she could breathe. Apart from breathing and trembling, she lay motionless.

I slid down the slope to help Clayton. We removed the snow from Popeye's upper side. Clayton went to her tail and pulled to encourage the horse to get to her feet. She was unhurt, so far as we could tell. I brushed snow from her and stroked her to comfort her.

Popeye tried to rise but could not. Either a leg was broken or the packbox on her lower side held her down.

We removed the packbox on top and released the saddle cinch. Without her load and packsaddle, Popeye was able to struggle to her feet. She stood quivering. I stroked her and told her what a fine little horse she was.

Clayton opened the packbox that held the two gallons of cod liver oil that the Indian Agent had sent. The bottles had been put on the very bottom of the box. They were unbroken. Nothing else in the load was breakable, except perhaps for my portable typewriter. We were not as immediately concerned about its condition as we were about the oil.

We fashioned tump lines from the pack ropes and struggled uphill with the packboxes. At the top we found that my saddlehorse had disappeared. While Clayton slid back down the slope to lead the packhorse out to the trail, I hiked back on Dream's tracks. She was standing at Jack Weldon's gate. Apparently she did not like the

Precipice Trail.

Eventually we had our three horses back at the dangerous place on the trail. We repacked Popeye. Her load was not heavy; a man could have carried it. Clayton tied a long rope to her halter and put a wrap on his saddlehorn. With steady tension on the rope, Popeye fearfully made her way around the bulging snowdrift.

Dream, fully sharp-shod, walked by without difficulty. I was not in the saddle, though. I was walking behind.

Three hours behind schedule, we gained the plateau. For the rest of the day we rode through miles of monotonous snow-covered jackpine forest, following a groove in the snow that indicated the trail.

The air became colder. The low yellow sun had no effect other than to highlight the frost crystals that drifted from the clear sky. The wilderness was silent but for the swish of the horses' legs through the dry snow and sudden rifle-like reports from trees cracking explosively in the cold.

Steam rose from the horses into the still air, and the hair on their bellies and chests was covered with frost. Clayton and I walked from time to time to get warm. But to cover the country at any speed we had to ride; the horses could move through deep snow much faster than we could.

The weak sun out-travelled us; it does not have far to go in midwinter. Our three-hour delay in the morning forced us to ride into the night. In the darkness of the forest, Popeye lost sight of Clayton's horse. The packhorse stopped and uttered a plaintive whinny. Dream collided with her. I shouted to Clayton. He called back. Popeye, oriented again, trudged ahead. The performance was enacted again and again in the dark.

To break the monotony, I remarked to Clayton, "At least we won't starve if we have to camp."

"What you mean?"

"We have two gallons of cod liver oil."

"Maybe I starve."

Not far to our right a wolf howled. It was answered by a wolf on our left. I was haunted by the wolf stories I had heard two evenings running at Atnarko and the Precipice.

I was becoming frightfully cold. My senses seemed deadened except for hearing. The steady swish, swish of dry snow against the horse's legs sounded loud. Crack! Frost split a tree. The wolves howled again—well behind us. I was dreadfully cold.

Suddenly Clayton reined his horse off the trail into untrodden snow. I was alarmed. A trail, however faint, connects you to other human beings. Off-trail there is only the encircling, indifferent wilderness.

"Where are you going, Clayton?" I cried.

"We take Natsadalia Trail. Shorter. We don't go to Anahim Lake this time."

We soon broke from the jackpine forest. Across an expanse of snow a pale light shone from a low building.

"My friend place. We make it," said Clayton, as though there had been some doubt in his mind.

I was too cold to speak.

A man shoved open the cabin door at the sound of our horses. "Who is it?"

"It me, Clayton."

"By God, you are riding late, Clayton. You must be gut-shrunk; your horses too. Come in and surround some grub. You can't ride hungry in such cold weather."

We turned our horses into a corral. Clayton's friend threw them some hay. We went into the cabin. At the doorway moist air struck us, and a thin fog of ice crystals formed.

"You bring cold weather, Clayton."

"I think you send it down to us."

"Where'd you ride from today?"

"We stay last night at Precipice. Start early, but packhorse slide off trail. She go long way down, end up under snow, nearly smother. It take nearly three hour to get straighten around. That why we ride late."

We drank tea heavy with sugar and ate bannock and strawberry jam, giving in return stories we had heard at Atnarko and the Precipice, information about deer, moose, wolves and the trail, and an elaborated account of Popeye's descent from the Precipice.

Clayton and I stood beside the heater, alternately facing it and turning our backs to it until our clothes scorched. I felt incurably cold. Gradually the warm cabin and the hot tea thawed us out.

I knew that Clayton had decided it was time to continue our journey when he looked slyly at his friend and said, "I damn near frost my pedal extremities today."

"What did you say?"

"I say I frost my pedal extremities, just about."

"It sounds more like you frosted your brain," his friend replied. He turned to me. "What is your Indian friend talking about?"

"A bicycle, maybe," I said hopefully.

The man frowned. "You guys are loony."

"I just want you to know that you are talking to a educated Indian," said Clayton. "I was teached by those smart Edwards brothers at Atnarko."

"You don't need education in this country," declared his friend. "What you need in this country is brains."

Reluctant as we were to face the cold, we had to do more riding that night. It was only two miles to the ranch house at Andy Christensen's Clesspocket Ranch. But the ride was across a broad meadow into a light but bitterly cold breeze. The cold air found its way through every seam in our clothes and stole all the heat we had absorbed in the cabin.

Dorothy Christensen answered my knock on the ranch house door. "Welcome, welcome," she said. "We had given up hope of seeing you today. Andy is busy at the moment."

We stood just inside the door in a thin cloud that condensed from our clothes, immensely grateful for warmth once again.

Andy Christensen called from another room. "Come in here, boys."

We padded across the floor in our moccasins. Andy was indeed busy. He was winning a poker game. The other two men in the room

Distributing hay to cattle at Clesspocket Ranch.

Dorothy Christensen
with pet sheep at
Clesspocket Ranch.

already knew Clayton. Andy introduced me to Billy Dagg and Louis Squinas.

"These boys just rode in from Bella Coola," explained Andy.

Louis Squinas laid down his cards and looked at us in apparent admiration. "Delate hyiu skookum tumtum, by gosh," he said in Chinook. Then he picked up his cards and added under his breath, "Damn fools." In Chinook we were very brave; in English we were damn fools. Louis Squinas could express himself also in Bella Coola and Carrier. He was a descendant of a Bella Coola Indian family which had established itself at Anahim Lake before white men arrived. He styled himself "a big gamble man."

Andy bundled into heavy clothes and went outside with us. We unpacked Popeye and set the packboxes indoors. Then we led the horses to the barn and watered and fed them.

Back at the ranch house Andy raised his lantern to read the thermometer on the doorpost. It registered thirty-five degrees below zero.

"I think you had better stay with us until it warms up a little," he said.

By next morning the mercury in the thermometer had sunk below the numbers on the scale.

"One thermometer alone can't handle this climate," Andy Christensen said. "We have to hook them up in tandem."

Andy and Dorothy Christensen were unusually refined individuals for the Anahim Lake country. Until recently he had been a storekeeper at Bella Coola. He looked the part too. He wore gold-rimmed glasses and tweed suits, and smoked cigars. Dorothy's quiet voice and gentle manner contrasted with the rough characters who inhabited the frontier. She was the daughter of John Clayton, who had bought the Hudson's Bay Company trading post at Bella Coola and made a fortune in land, fish and furs. She was Clayton Mack's half-aunt; her father was Clayton Mack's grandfather.

The Christensens had moved from Bella Coola to Anahim Lake at the beginning of the depression, choosing the hard climate of the plateau over the gentle one in the valley. They ran five hundred cattle

158

on the best meadows in the region which Dorothy's father had bought years earlier. With beef on the hoof worth two cents a pound, hardly any rancher was making money. Perhaps Andy Christensen had calculated that neither his Bella Coola store nor his Anahim Lake ranch was a paying proposition in hard times—unless they were put together as a unit. In any case, he trailed beef from Anahim Lake directly to his butcher shop in Bella Coola and made a profit. He brought back goods to trade with the Indians for furs and made a profit again. His twenty-horse pack outfit was continually on the trail. Besides, he was filling the trade vacuum left by the death of Antoine Capoose, the notorious Carrier Indian trader.

Clayton returned to his ranch at nearby Abuntlet Lake. I tried to earn my keep at Clesspocket Ranch by pitching hay and cutting wood. I accompanied the sleigh that left the barn each day heaped with hay, swinging slowly across the meadow in great loops, depositing piles of hay first from one side, then from the other. A stream of white-faced cattle followed the sleigh. Half a dozen at a time halted at each pile of hay. A cold sun cast long shadows across the snow.

I was advised against travelling alone in search of my lost horse in cold weather. If I became lost or my saddlehorse deserted me, I would not survive a long walk back to the ranch. The only securely warm creatures in the country were Dorothy Christensen's heavily woolled pet sheep, and they had the good sense to stay inside their shed.

A week passed before the thermometer began to rise a little. Outlying frontiersmen began to take an interest in something other than feeding stoves and stock. Some of them made long rides to Andy Christensen's ranch for poker games, a few purchases at the store serving to excuse the trip. Many of the men were of mixed blood, a natural consequence of young white men arriving in the country unmarried. The mixed-blood people were tough, good-humoured models of fortitude. Much of the heavy ranch work fell to them. Their winter sports were poker, coyote hunting and wild horse chasing.

Only in winter were riders able to catch wild horses. The horses were half-starved and weak if snow came early and lay deep, especially if there had been a thaw and a freeze. This put a glaze of ice on the snow through which horses could not paw for grass. Then men mounted on well-fed horses could run the wild ones to a standstill. Even then it took a strong horse and a brave rider to crash through spruce and pine thickets and across rough, frozen bogs in hot pursuit. Wild horses were fast and cunning, and they knew the country.

Official open season on wild horses in the plateau country was from January 1 to May 1. All domestic stock had to be off the open range or risk being shot. The government bounty on wild horses was five dollars for mares and seven and a half dollars for stallions. Hunters had to be licensed before they were permitted to shoot wild horses. To prove their kills, they had to produce ears from the horses, plus genitals from the stallions.

Sometimes there was more profit in taking feral horses alive. After halter-breaking them, a horse hunter might receive eight or ten dollars each for the animals. Not all wild horses could be taken alive. Some were too wily to be caught; others fought to the death against captivity. In one case a wild horse was roped after a full day's chase; the terrified animal emitted a final high squeal and dropped dead on the spot.

Coyote hunting was not as hard on horses and riders as wild horse chasing and paid better. In fact, coyote pelts probably paid the bills of many frontier ranchers who had no cattle to sell while they built up their herds. A coyote pelt might bring fifteen or twenty dollars, a lot of money to a rancher who otherwise made ends meet by eating moose meat and wearing homemade moosehide clothing.

Successful coyote hunting depended on snow conditions which might occur only for a day or two in a winter—or perhaps for a month or two. Ideal conditions were powdery snow deep enough to cause coyotes to lunge through it but not deep enough to slow a strong horse.

A mounted hunter, club in hand, searched snow-covered

meadows for fresh tracks of coyotes hunting for mice. When he spotted a coyote, the rider spurred his mount to a gallop. A fast horse could exhaust a coyote in ten or fifteen minutes in soft snow. Once the coyote had been run to a standstill, the hunter clubbed it to death. If a coyote reached the forest at the edge of the meadow, it escaped. A fast attack was essential.

When the temperature climbed to twenty-five degrees below zero, Lester Dorsey, one of the poker players, suggested, "Let's go coyoting tomorrow if it don't snow."

Mac McEwan, a slow-talking man of mixed blood, turned to me and said, "You . . . can . . . come . . . with . . . me . . . to . . . see . . . . what . . . it . . . is . . . like." Mac spoke so slowly I wondered how he could match speed with the coyotes.

"Your . . . horses . . . are . . . no . . . good . . . for . . . coyoting," he drawled. "One . . . is . . . too . . . big . . . and . . . one . . . is . . . too . . . fat. I . . . will . . . lend . . . you . . . one . . . of . . . mine."

My mind was spinning at top speed in anticipation of the hunt. Mac's slow drawl drove me to distraction. I found myself finishing his sentences for him.

In the morning Mac loaned me a pair of warm moosehide chaps and a wiry, medium-sized cayuse eager for the chase. For a few miles we followed the sleigh road that went to Ulkatcho. "No . . . good . . . . to . . . follow . . . broke . . . trail," Mac said eventually.

We began to skirt the edge of a meadow. "Got . . . to . . . stay . . . . between . . . coyote . . . and . . . trees. Keep . . . him . . . in . . . the . . . open . . . and . . . run . . . him . . . down."

I gripped a club in my right hand and reins in my left. I studied the snow for coyote tracks. The meadow was crisscrossed by moose tracks.

Mac reined his horse to a halt. Surprisingly quickly, he said, "Over there!"

I searched the meadow with my eyes and eventually spotted a grey animal jumping in a leisurely way through the snow.

Mac said, "Let's go."

We spurred our horses into a gallop. Heads low, manes flying,

Trading coyote furs at Bert Lehman's trading post just east of Anahim Lake.

the horses closed in on the grey animal. It stopped a moment, then fled to the trees. Snow flew from the horses' hooves in clouds of crystals.

My horse struck a frozen hummock at top speed, stumbled and fell. I flew from the saddle and ploughed through the snow.

I lay still for moments, unable to breathe. I began to gasp. The wind had been knocked out of me. My nose was full of snow. I rolled over, face up, took off a glove and scraped snow from my face. I lay pillowed in the snow. I felt defeated.

Two horses trotted up. Mac was leading mine.

"Look . . . like . . . you . . . get . . . throwed. Are . . . you . . . hurt?"

"No, just shaken up."

"I . . . look . . . back . . . and . . . see . . . your . . . horse . . . hunting . . . coyote . . . on . . . his . . . own."

"The horse threw me. I suppose the coyote got away."

"It . . . Louis's . . . dog. Look . . . lot . . . like . . . coyote."

The meadows near Abuntlet Lake revealed fresh tracks but no coyotes. In the afternoon we joined the Ulkatcho sleigh road and headed back to Clesspocket Ranch.

"I . . . shoulda . . . hit . . . Louis's . . . dog," drawled Mac. "Then . . . we . . . not . . . be . . . skunked."

"We all lived to hunt another day: Louis's dog, the coyotes and me," I summed up. "As for me, I am going to leave swamp meadows, fast horses and coyotes to you Anahim Lake cowboys."

The mercury had stuck in the thermometer at twenty-five degrees below zero. Small snowflakes emerged reluctantly from unmottled clouds. The weather was right for delivering cod liver oil.

I set out with Dream and Popeye again, the two jars of cod liver oil in gunny sacks tied to the horn of my riding saddle; I didn't want to have to unpack Popeye at Anahim Lake. I presented the jars to the Indian Health Nurse, remarking that cod liver oil was one more incomprehensible gift of the white man to the Indians.

From Anahim Lake I headed east to a trading post run by Stanley Dowling and Bert Lehman. Stan Dowling had arrived flat broke in the Anahim Lake country three years previously. While earning a few dollars haying for Andy Christensen and Lester Dorsey, he had observed how slow and expensive packtrains, sleighs and wagons were for moving supplies to Anahim Lake from Bella Coola and Williams Lake. Even though the road ended at Towdystan twenty miles away he decided to acquire a truck. In the fall of 1936, with a hundred and fifteen dollars in his pocket, he rode away from Anahim Lake. He returned with a second-hand truck and three tons of goods. He had winched and jacked the truck through mudholes and chopped his way over jackpine ridges to Anahim Lake.

Stan Dowling threw in with Bert Lehman, who had come into the country at about the same time. Bert had a dozen or so cattle and horses and a twenty-foot by twenty-foot log cabin. The men divided the building into a store and living quarters. In a short time they had sold the first truckload of goods.

When I arrived Stan Dowling was in Vancouver buying more merchandise. With Stan away, there was room for me to bunk at the trading post while I searched for my horse.

The trading post, six miles east of the Squinas place at Anahim Lake, was a meeting place for the young men who were setting up ranches in the surrounding country. To it came all the news of the Anahim Lake region, the normal frontier talk of horses, horse trades, recently discovered meadows, meadows for sale, home brew nearly ready, imminent game warden patrols, newcomers to the country, wild horse sightings, wolves, moose hunts and amusing stories about somebody's misadventures, especially in horse and equipment trading.

I was sure that everyone in the country knew what had become of my horse Peanuts. But nobody let on. They were going to let me find out for myself—while providing me with the greatest hospitality. Somebody casually mentioned that he thought he saw a horse that looked something like the one I described being ridden by an Indian near Nimpo Lake. It was as close as anyone came to being forthright. I began to suspect that Peanuts had been a wild card in some elaborate horse trades that many people had a hand in.

I saddled Dream and set out for an Indian settlement near Nimpo Lake. It was a bright day, only a little below zero Fahrenheit. The sleigh road was well-packed. I rode along squinting into the low sun, happy finally to be following a clue in the mystery of my missing horse.

About noon I pulled up to a cluster of four log cabins that had woodsmoke rising straight up from the chimneys. Except for a baby crying, the place was quiet.

I knocked on the door of the nearest cabin. There was a long silence. Then the door opened a crack. A pair of intensely dark eyes in a brown face peered out.

"I'm looking for a horse," I blurted out before the door could close.

"Horse," repeated the man.

"Yes, a small, brown gelding. All brown, just a little white on his face."

The man was silent a moment. Then he said, "I trade that gelding Ulkatcho man. No good that horse."

"It was a good horse the last I saw it. Where is it now?"

"Dead now."

"Dead!"

"That little gelding die Itcha Mountain. No good that horse. Chase wild horse just little, he die."

"So you ran him to death chasing wild horses."

The door closed.

I swung aboard Dream, wheeled her about and started back to Bert Lehman's store at a trot. I felt heavy with sadness.

The weak sun sank behind the mountains to the southwest. Night settled under the trees. A gibbous moon sailed high, replacing the sun's yellow light with reflected white. Cold came with the white light, piercing my wool coat and stinging my nose.

Half an hour from the trading post, I saw black objects flitting among the moon shadows under the trees. They were much too small for horses or moose. Maybe they were deer—but that was improbable. Suddenly it dawned upon me: they were wolves.

There was nothing I could do but sit in the saddle and let Dream move ahead. Trying to break the tension I felt, I attempted to sing. After a few croaks I settled on "Hi, ho, hey diddly diddly," repeated over and over with slight variations. The wolves disappeared into the shadows. Probably they had never before heard anything so ridiculous. Certainly I had not. It did not begin to compare with their own melodious singing.

Lester Dorsey and Andy Holte were visiting Bert Lehman when I arrived at the trading post.

"I heard you was looking for a horse," said Andy. "Find him?"

"No," I replied dejectedly. "He is dead, run to death chasing wild horses."

"Who done it?" asked Lester.

"An Indian down toward Nimpo Lake told me an Ulkatcho man did it. But I think he did it himself."

"You are lucky you come back yourself," said Lester. "That bunch is cultus."

"Well, I survived—and I came across wolves close up on the way back too."

Lester's eyes brightened. "You don't say. I will look for their tracks in the morning. I could use some bounty money."

"Can I go along and help you chase them?" I asked. I added with a disparaging chuckle, "I am an experienced coyote hunter, you know."

Lester smiled his slow smile. "I heard about Mac pulling you feet first out of a snowbank. That ain't the kind of experience you need for hunting wolves. You can't chase wolves on horseback. Snow don't hold wolves back none. They are too strong. They barrel through snow like a train and are in the timber before you get anywheres near 'em. Bullets, traps and poison are what it takes for them brutes!"

The loss of Peanuts persuaded me to give up owning horses at all. I did not need them any more. Bella Coola was not horse country and I had decided to make the valley my home.

Giving up my buckskin mare Dream was as painful as losing Peanuts. Both horses had shared trails with me through the Rocky Mountains and across British Columbia. Dream was the last of the five horses that had accompanied me on my four-month journey from Alberta to Bella Coola in 1933.

Horse and equipment trading was the favourite occupation of the Anahim Lake ranchers. I would be at a great disadvantage in negotiating with them. I had observed Bert Lehman's fair dealing in his store. Also, I assumed that a man who laughed at the top of his lungs most of the time would not be underhanded. I asked him to sell my horses for me.

Andy Holte was one of the keenest horse traders in the Anahim Lake country. He told me, "I heard about that Dream buckskin of yours. She might do me for a spare."

"A spare!" exploded Bert Lehman. He was already bargaining for me. "Anyone who doesn't use a horse like that as a regular mount doesn't know a good horse when he sees one."

"I ain't seen the horse. I only heard about it," Andy defended himself. "Anyways, I do not need another horse bad. I just got myself a Sugar Loaf Mountain horse today, that spooky bay that come in tied behind my sleigh. That horse is the best ever sired out of a mare."

Bert guffawed. "There is no need to tell us how good your new Sugar Loaf Mountain horse is, Andy. We are not trading for it. We are trading for the Bella Coola buckskin."

Andy Holte was keyed up about his Sugar Loaf Mountain horse; he could not be contained. "That Sugar Loaf Mountain horse will be worth any two in the country. She just needs to be broke. Tomorrow I will get you fellas to help me harness her."

In the morning half a dozen Indians came to the trading post with furs. They left with wool sweaters, moccasin rubbers, tea, sugar, tobacco and rifle shells. No cash was exchanged.

"Figured I might get enough money from that bunch to buy your little blind-one-side bay mare," said Bert. "But they traded furs, and the rest was jawbone. Furs, jawbone, horses and equipment trades: who needs money at Anahim Lake?" His thunderous laugh rattled a stack of tobacco tins.

Andy Holte inspected Dream. He came inside and said, "I will give you my team for that Dream horse."

Bert Lehman roared; I could count the fillings in his teeth. "Andy, horse trading is one thing; horse theft is something else. It is unneighbourly to try to unload your nags for the best saddlehorse you ever saw."

Andy reflected a moment. "Bert, I have to meet Stan with my sleigh at Kleena Kleene and bring in your truckload of iktahs. I cannot stay here haggling all day. When I get back I will give you all three horses I have here for the buckskin. By that time the Sugar Loaf

Mountain horse will be broke to harness real good."

"That Sugar Loaf Mountain horse don't impress no one but you, Andy," said Bert. "Nobody knows how it will turn out. It is a pig in a poke."

"I will throw in the harness."

Bert Lehman guffawed loudly.

"All I got left to offer is my sleigh."

"That might do, Andy. You have a fine team and sleigh, but they are just ordinary. I hesitate to trade something special for something ordinary. But it might do."

I was open-mouthed at Bert's bargaining. Andy seemed to agree with his evaluation of Dream. "I will talk more about this horse when I get back with Stanley's load," he said. He pulled his wool cap down over his bald head. "Now I will request the assistance of you gentlemen in the harnessing of my ordinary team and my extraordinary Sugar Loaf Mountain horse."

Andy Holte led his horses from the barn. One of the gentle ones was placed on the right side of the tongue of the sleigh, and the unbroken horse was placed on the left side.

The wild one was jittery and nervous when the harness went on. The tugs were hooked shorter on him so that he would do most of the pulling. A rope was tied from his halter to the hame of his experienced partner. All was ready. Bert held the horses.

Andy climbed onto the box of the sleigh and stood up. He shouted, "Let's go, you bog trotters!" He snapped the rump of the unbroken horse with the reins. It plunged ahead, kicking and squalling. The sleigh performed a big arc around the meadow, throwing up a cloud of snow. The wild horse was doing most of the pulling; the other horse was merely running with it. Whenever the unbroken horse slackened its pace, Andy Holte hollered and snapped the reins. In not many minutes the sleigh pulled up in front of the trading post.

"He's broke now," Andy grinned. "Them Sugar Loaf Mountain horses do learn fast."

I made a formal agreement with Bert Lehman to sell my two

horses. Then I rented a horse from him to ride across the Chilcotin as far as Tatla Lake. Bert said, "When you get to Tatla Lake, take off the bridle and tie it to the saddle and turn the horse loose. It will come right home."

I was only a hundred miles from Bella Coola, but to get there the way I had come would entail a lonely ride in arctic weather on trails hidden by snow. The trip would be trying at best, fatal if bad weather or bad luck camped on my trail. On the way up I had depended on Clayton Mack's knowledge of the country.

In any case I wanted to see the Chilcotin. I would ride horseback to Tatla Lake, then take the mail truck to Williams Lake, the Pacific Great Eastern Railway to Squamish, Union Steamship to Vancouver and finally Union Steamship again to Bella Coola: eight hundred miles against one hundred, but safer.

The thermometer on Bert Lehman's doorpost read twenty-eight below zero. It was too cold to ride. I climbed onto the sleigh beside Andy Holte and covered myself with blankets. My rented horse and one of Andy's were tied to the rear of the sleigh. The wild one and an experienced horse were harnessed in front.

Andy slapped the reins on the team's rumps and shouted. We started off with a lurch. I looked back at Dream and felt like a betrayer. I did not know for sure who her next owner might be. She stood calmly in front of the trading post, hiding little Popeye from my view.

I felt a surge of empathy for the wild horse from Sugar Loaf Mountain pulling the sleigh at full tilt, fighting the harness. It fought against its fate. Eventually the wild horse slowed to a steady walk, giving the other horse some pulling to do. But from time to time through the day it rebelled and broke into a run. Exhaustion was its only reward.

In the afternoon we pulled into Tom and Annie Engebretson's place at Towdystan near the headwaters of the Dean River. Tom was away at a hay camp feeding cattle. Annie and two sons held down the home ranch. She was the daughter of Halvor Jakob Johnson Lunos who had acquired the square mile of crown grant land at

Towdystan at the turn of the century. Tom Engebretson became part of the family ranch when he married Annie. They drove their cattle to market at Bella Coola over the Lunos Trail to the Precipice and then over the Sugar Camp Trail to Atnarko.

In the morning the temperature was forty below zero, too cold to travel. We stayed at Towdystan for another day. Annie Engebretson told us about George Turner, with whom we would stay next. George Turner had come into the Chilcotin a little later than Annie Engebretson's father and settled at Kleena Kleene some thirty miles east of Towdystan. For a long time he did not use his name enough to keep a shine on it. He was probably an American but he revealed nothing about his past. This provoked speculation and gossip, but the frontier settlers did not inquire directly into each other's lives. Trying to put scarce facts into a pattern, the neighbours noted that George Turner had appeared at Kleena Kleene not long after the Dalton Brothers, a notorious gang of Kansas bank robbers, had come to a violent end. Four members had been killed in a gun fight, Emmett Dalton had been captured and one member had escaped. Emmett Dalton was released after fourteen years in prison. Soon after, in 1914 or so, a man showed up outside the Engebretson ranch house where George Turner was visiting. The stranger and George Turner had a violent argument outside the house. The stranger departed.

It was not much to go on. There was a further, unrelated mystery that touched George Turner's life. One day somebody shot the Chilcotin Indian chief One Eye dead. George Turner had eloped with One Eye's daughter; the chief had disapproved of the marriage.

The temperature warmed up to thirty below zero the next day. Andy Holte and I harnessed the team and continued our journey. The sleigh slid across Caribou Flats and down the break at McClinchy Hill to McClinchy Creek, a tributary of the Klinaklini River. At the river, near One Eye Lake, we turned into the George Turner place.

We were welcomed into a large, new log home by Old George Turner and his son Young George Turner. Young George was strikingly handsome. He had a cute three-year-old daughter. We

George Turner, Senior, who some neighbours believed was an escaped member of the Dalton Gang.

were not introduced to an old woman who sat on the floor, her knees drawn up under her chin, mumbling to herself.

Old George Turner cooked venison steaks and onions for supper. I wondered about Young George Turner's wife and particularly about his sister Mary Ann who was reputed to be as beautiful as her brother was handsome. Conforming to local custom, I refrained from asking questions in the George Turner household.

Early in the evening the outside door creaked open. A pair of dark eyes scrutinized us. Then a beautiful woman of mixed blood moved shyly but gracefully into the room. Old George Turner introduced his daughter. She said hello and disappeared into another room.

171

Ralph and
Harold
Sculthorpe.

Andy Holte was going to wait for Stanley Dowling and his truck at Turner's place. The temperature had climbed a little more. I could risk riding on alone with my rented horse.

Before leaving I asked permission to take a photograph of Young George Turner's little daughter. Then, with some trepidation, I asked Old George if I might take a picture of him. He agreed readily. I wondered if a true member of the Dalton Gang would be so gracious. On the other hand, a refusal could have fuelled the surmises of which the old man must have been aware.

At noon I stopped at the home of Sam Colwell, the telegraph operator. He gave me letters to take to Tatla Lake to put on the weekly mail truck, and his wife gave me an excellent lunch. I moved on, filling the short day with travel.

Even on the high plateau in cloudless weather, the January day was not long enough to get me to Tatla Lake. The sun was tucking itself in for the night when I came upon a cabin. The door was unlocked. I entered. The cabin was warm. What had appeared at first to be timely shelter perhaps was not; it would depend on the hospitality of the occupants.

I placed a few sticks of wood on the winking coals in the stove. Before long two young men burst through the door. They immediately introduced themselves as Ralph and Harold Sculthorpe. They looked much alike except for their hair styles. Ralph had a bald front and a short-cropped back. Harold's hair stared in all directions. Flipped upside down, Harold could have been used to wash out large bottles.

The customs of the country required that they invite me to stay. When I expressed my gratitude, Harold asked his brother, "How many?"

Ralph replied, "Two."

In a few minutes Harold returned with two headless chickens dripping blood.

The Sculthorpe brothers were engaging hosts, talkative and jocular. They were novice trappers, full of amusing stories about the sort of misadventures that do not befall experienced woodsmen. They had been forced back to their roadside cabin by inadvertently burning down their spruce bough bivouac at the head of the Klinaklini River.

I reached Graham's ranch at Tatla Lake in the afternoon the next day. I took the bridle off Bert Lehman's horse and fastened it to the saddle. Then I slapped the mare on her rump and said, "Home you go, old girl." She started up the road at a trot. She would be home the following day; it was only fifty miles.

I walked toward Tatla Lake Lodge with my sleeping bag and camera in one arm and my portable typewriter in the other. I was no longer a horseman. I was a pedestrian with an IOU for two horses in my pocket and in my heart regrets for a third that lay dead in the snow in the Itcha Mountains.

I went down to the basement where Bob and Margaret Graham lived in cold weather. The mail truck from Williams Lake had just arrived. Mail and freight for the entire west Chilcotin and the Tatlayoko Lake country was being sorted.

In the morning I started for Williams Lake in the Hodgson's Truck Line truck with Fred Linder driving. Except for snow drifts the road was good. We covered a hundred and fifty miles in two days, the fastest I had travelled in months. We stayed overnight at Lee's Lodge at Alexis Creek.

At Williams Lake the Pacific Great Eastern Railway steam locomotive was throwing off steam in a way that reminded me of the cloud of snow Andy Holte's team had raised on the meadow at Anahim Lake.

I commented to a man in the waiting room that if the PGE had built a branch line to Bella Coola, as once was proposed, I would have had a short and easy trip home.

"It would take longer on the PGE," the man said.

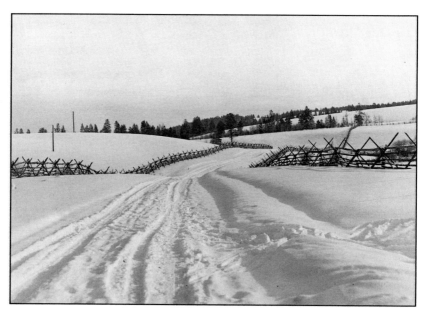

The Chilcotin Road lined with Russell fences.

Interlude Three

In 1937 I acquired a boat and a wife. I was courting when I bought the boat, so I named it *Beegie* which stood for Best Girl. The name was equivocal enough to obviate a change if things did not work out. As it happened, they did. I should have named the boat *Mae*.

Mae Edwards and Gladys Edwards on the *Beegie* at Bella Coola.

The boat was a thirty-foot west coast gillnetter with a one-cylinder Easthope marine engine but without a gillnet drum. I used the gasboat for living quarters while I held down the job of fishery guardian at Kwatna Inlet west of Bella Coola.

Near the end of August I headed for Bella Coola at top speed—six knots with a following westerly—and married Mae Edwards in Mackenzie United Church. My bride and I started for Kwatna that very afternoon for a honeymoon to be paid for by the Department of Fisheries. Lord Tweedsmuir, the Governor-General of Canada, was in Bella Coola at the time, inaugurating Tweedsmuir Provincial Park and the Tweedsmuir Trail. I was too wrapped up in my own social affairs to partake in his.

In 1938 I put a gillnet drum on the *Beegie,* hoping to earn big money as a commercial fisherman. It was a poor season—even experienced fishermen did not do well. For a prairie boy who did not know the habits of salmon, it was a financial disaster.

On July 2 my wife delivered a son. Domestic responsibilities were crowding me. I was desperate for an income. Memories of the small money I had earned at writing and photography loomed large. I fled to the wilderness one more time for stories, photographs—and adventure.

Through Tweedsmuir Park
by Packhorse and *Lily*

"Happy, happy days were these—days the memory of which goes very far into the future, growing brighter as we journey farther away from them, for the scenes through which our course was laid were such as speak in whispers, only when we have left them—the whispers of the pine-tree, the music of running water, the stillness of great lonely lakes."

William Francis Butler, The Great Lone Land

Joe Cahoose and Harold Giles fording the Dean River west of Ulkatcho.

TWEEDSMUIR PARK 1938

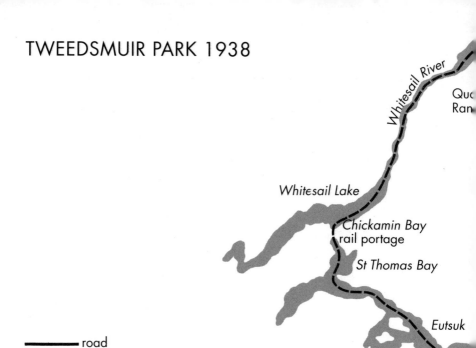

Whitesail River

Qu[...]
Ran[...]

Whitesail Lake

Chickamin Bay
rail portage

St Thomas Bay

Eutsuk

——— road

- - - - route travelled

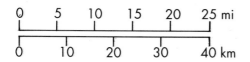

| 0 | 5 | 10 | 15 | 20 | 25 mi |

| 0 | 10 | 20 | 30 | 40 km |

N

Dean
River

Dean

Channel

Dean

Bella Coola R

Bella Coola

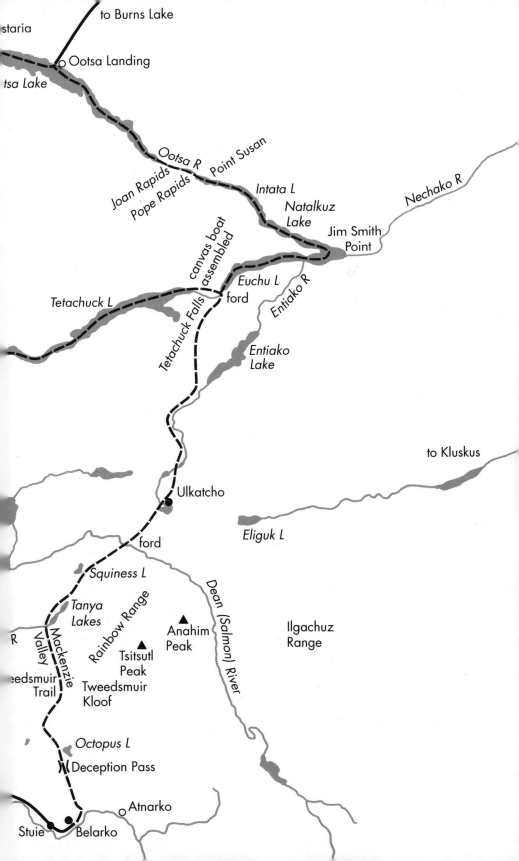

I PUT THE IDEA OF A HORSEBACK TRIP OVER the new Tweedsmuir Trail and a boat trip through the lakes of Tweedsmuir Park to Harold Giles. He was a schoolteacher whose summers were free. Harold liked the idea. My wife was aghast.

The boat was a collapsible canoe made of rubberized canvas stretched over a folding wooden frame. It had been used by Viking Timber Company timber cruisers. When the company went broke, it became part payment on a bad debt owed to the Northcop Logging Company. The company accountant admitted that the canoe was too old to be of use to timber cruisers. Nevertheless, he wanted a deposit to cover its replacement value. "I need something to show on the books if you don't come back," he said. The boat was named *Lily* after the timber cruiser's wife who had been wide in the middle and narrow at both ends.

On August 4 Harold and I trucked our gear to the end of the road near Barney Brynildsen's farm at Belarko. Joe Cahoose, an Ulkatcho Indian, waited there with three saddlehorses and two packhorses. Joe rode a gelding he called Maly Jane, but otherwise his outfit was conventional. I was pleased with it.

The collapsed canoe was bulky and awkward to pack. We finally got it lashed down. Joe called the horse that carried the canoe the steamboat horse. The kitchen horse carried our grub and cooking gear. Sleeping bags and odds and ends went behind our riding saddles. We had three guns: Joe's .32 Special, my .22 and Harold's Watkins Fly Spray gun.

We started up the Tweedsmuir Trail at four o'clock in the afternoon, a time of day when I usually look for a stopping place for the night. Harold and I had hired Joe Cahoose but we soon learned that it was Joe Cahoose who would make the decisions. "My horse he gotta go make hay Anahim Lake," he said to explain his impatience. He also resented Brynildsen's twenty-five cent per day horse grazing fee on an overgrazed pasture.

The upshot was that we camped on the mountainside with the horses tied to trees. None of us had been over the trail before. We had hoped that a patch of grass would appear before dark. It did not.

The Tweedsmuir Trail was a gentle trail compared to others in the country but it was too narrow to camp on. No fire, no water, no tent, horses tied to trees: it was hardly a camp. We went to bed without supper.

We packed at daybreak and rode over the rim of the valley into rolling, forested country. Near Bear Camp Creek a small wet meadow appeared. We stopped, unloaded the kitchen horse, let the horses loose to feed and cooked a double ration of bacon and eggs. We hit the trail a couple of hours later full of pep.

On the way to Deception Pass the scenery was unremarkable until at the pass the world spread out before us. We stopped to pick out familiar landmarks. The Coast Mountains thrust jagged peaks at the sky in the northwest. Due north were the rounded red summits of the Rainbow Mountains. Mount Waddington, the highest peak in British Columbia, rose above lesser peaks far to the south.

While Harold and I admired the scenery, Joe shot and skinned

Harold Giles at Stuie, August 1, 1938.

a marmot that had made the mistake of whistling within rifle shot.

As we lingered in the pass we observed a dozen or so riders leave the timber below. When the riders neared the top of the pass we slid our horses down a snowbank to meet them.

The horseman in the lead was George Draney. Behind him were a dozen women, participants in the inaugural ride of the Tweedsmuir Park Trail Riders. They had left Tweedsmuir Lodge on July 29 and had one more night on the trail.

In association with the Union Steamship Company, Tommy Walker, owner of Tweedsmuir Lodge at Stuie, had arranged a twelve-day tour. The tourists took a two-day cruise from Vancouver to Bella Coola on the SS *Cardena*, rode for seven days on a packhorse trip into the Rainbow Mountains and then returned to Vancouver on the ship—all for eighty-five dollars.

George Draney was a soft-spoken gentleman and an excellent horseman. He wrangled the dudes. His brother Bob was equally good with horses. He wrangled the packhorses. The difference between the brothers was that even in ordinary circumstances Bob's language skirted the margins of acceptability for schoolmarms and stenographers. While dealing with packhorses, Bob had to be kept out of earshot to protect the reputation of the Tweedsmuir Park Trail Riders.

Shortly after leaving George and his dozen, we came to Bob Draney and Joe Goff tightening the last diamond hitch on six packhorses. I asked Bob how he liked tending dudes. "They are not as savvy as horses," he said, "and they are trickier to herd." He added, "They figure they were misled by Tommy's advertising: not by what he said but by what he didn't say. He neglected to mention that the Rainbow Mountains have the worst mosquitoes in Canada."

Joe Cahoose was surprised to come across white women far back in the sticks. "Lotsa women that bunch," he noted. "Maybe some women stop, smoke skin."

"I don't think you'd get any of 'em to help you, Joe," said Bob Draney. "They are so saddle-sored and mosquito-bit that they talk only about getting back to the lodge and having a bath." He reflected

Joe Cahoose and Harold Giles descending the north side of
Deception Pass.

a moment. "Twelve baths in a row! Tommy's going to have to run
'em through the sheep dip."

Joe was puzzled. "Why they come this place? Ride all day. They
got lotsa money."

Bob Draney and Joe Goff strung the packhorses out at a fast
walk. They wanted to overtake the trail riders and set up a
comfortable camp at Bear Camp Creek before the riders got there.

Joe, Harold and I rode north to Octopus Lake, where Joe
insisted we stop. He wanted to cook his marmot and tan the skin.
We built three fires: one to smoke the marmot skin, one to roast the
marmot carcass and one for Harold and me to cook on.

As he scraped the skin, Joe muttered, "Woman job." He
suggested to me, "Maybe big chief get woman."

Joe was a skilful flatterer. Although he called me the big chief,
it was he who decided when we started in the morning and where
we stopped in the afternoon. It was he who relaxed by the fire while
Harold and I rustled wood and cooked meals.

Joe ate our bannock and beans, but it was evident that he was

183

impatient to tie into something more substantial, namely the marmot. Finally he pulled it from the skewer. He offered a piece of meat to Harold and to me. We gulped it down in deference. Joe devoured the rest of the marmot with gusto as though he had been starving on white man's fare.

Next morning while I was saddling a packhorse, the animal nipped me on the shoulder. I complained to Joe. "Maybe horse die, you pay me fifty dollar," he replied. Joe was careful to protect his investments.

We moved easily up the open alpine slope to the rim of Mackenzie Valley. A yearling mountain caribou trotted toward us, peered curiously and paced away. Two long ridges of rounded summits separated by a bright green valley stretched ahead of us. The treeless mountains were magnificently coloured purple, yellow, red and orange.

I turned to our packer. "What do the Indians call these mountains, Joe?"

"My daddy call him mountain who bleed," Joe said. He pointed to a yellow slope where a streak of red emerged like a flow of blood.

Joe seemed to have a premonition about the trail ahead. He did not want to lead. "Don't know this trail," he said.

"None of us do," I replied. "But it is the best trail in the country, built only last year for the governor-general."

Joe looked at me solemnly. "Chief always go first in new place."

"Whatever you want, Joe," I said. "I don't see what difference it makes who goes ahead."

I started my horse down the switchbacks into Mackenzie Valley. The animal shuddered and then bucked. It tossed me loose from the saddle. I lost a stirrup, grabbed a handful of mane and hung on. The horse clattered down the trail at breakneck speed. I pulled back on the reins and hollered, "Whoa, whoa!" The animal missed a switchback turn and we ended up in a patch of alpine fir. I stayed in the trees; the horse carried on.

Harold jumped from his horse, covered his head with his jacket and ran down the trail to where I lay. "Are you okay, Cliff?"

Joe Cahoose and Harold Giles packing the steamboat horse.

Joe Cahoose overlooking an unnamed lake in the Rainbow Mountains. The Tweedsmuir Trail goes over Deception Pass on the extreme left.

Joe Cahoose looking into Mackenzie Valley in the Rainbow Mountains.

Joe Cahoose and Harold Giles on the Tweedsmuir Trail.

"I don't know." I moved each arm, then each leg. "Everything seems to work."

"What's the trouble? Hornets?"

"Yes. That cunning Joe. He knew all along."

Joe led the packhorses well off the trail onto loose scree. When he reached Harold and me he explained. "No good yellowjacket bite kitchen horse and steamboat horse. More better he bite saddlehorse. Chief make good ride."

The excitement of the wasps over, my saddlehorse stood on the trail waiting for the other horses to catch up. I mounted and rode ahead into Mackenzie Valley. The floor of the valley was covered with mountain flowers. There seemed to be a competition of colour between the mountain peaks and the meadows.

This time I made the decision to stop and camp. I had serious photography to do.

Next morning we left behind the flamboyant colours of Mackenzie Valley and entered the subdued hues of spruce and pine forest. We skirted Tweedsmuir Kloof, a gorge that a creek had cut through the lava, then descended toward the valley containing Tanya Lake.

A grizzly bear stepped onto the trail and began to walk toward us, the silver fur over his shoulders rippling. I stopped my horse. The bear kept coming. He was not charging or huffing—he just seemed to have something on his mind. Then he stopped abruptly, rose on his hind legs, sniffed the air and crashed off the trail. My heart was pounding. I turned in my saddle and grinned weakly at Harold. "I should have had my camera ready."

Harold said calmly, "I believe he was frightened by the mingled odours of an Indian, a white man and a photographer."

Joe had his rifle free of its scabbard and gave only a relieved "by gosh."

The new Tweedsmuir Trail joined the old Ulkatcho Trail in a large meadow above the Takia River. About noon we splashed across the river and stepped out of our saddles in front of an Indian camp. The air was scented by woodsmoke and decaying fish guts. Rows of salmon fillets hung in the smokehouse. The fires were tended by an old Indian woman and a boy. Joe said a few words to the woman in Carrier and she replied. Joe interpreted for Harold and me, "Men catch fish in river and women pick berry."

"We are too late for breakfast and too early for the lahal game," I said. "Let's go ahead to the Dean River."

The trail to Dean River ran through level country with only Squiness Lake and a couple of cabins to break the monotony. The trail was being used heavily by packtrains carrying dried fish from Tanya Lake to Ulkatcho and Kluskus. There were few prospects for photography, so I set a fast pace. Joe had put me at the head of the packtrain. "Lotsa yellowjacket this place," he explained. I agreed that we did not want the packhorse carrying the canvas boat crashing through the forest to escape wasps. Joe Cahoose was pretty smart.

We forded the Dean River late in the afternoon and unpacked on the east bank. Joe picketed the horses in the meadow. Harold and I went to the river with fishing lines. Even duffers can catch trout in the Dean; we were determined to have rainbow trout for supper.

I went upstream; Harold went down. In fifteen minutes I had three large trout, enough for the three of us. There was no need to catch more. I was proud of my unaccustomed success as a fisherman but I did not want to embarrass Harold.

"Catch anything, Harold?" I called loudly.

The reply was a great splash a hundred feet away. I pushed through the willows to see Harold clambering onto the bank, soaking wet. On the bank were seven trout.

"What are you doing, Harold?" I demanded. "Are you pulling them out by hand?"

Harold looked sheepish. "I stepped onto the log to bring the last one in and I slipped off. I guess that ends the fishing in this pool."

I threw my three fish into his bunch to forestall comparisons about fishing ability. "We have plenty, anyway."

At camp Joe asked, "Lotsa fish?"

"I caught three trout and one Harold," I replied. "We'll cook the fish now and save Harold for an emergency."

Next morning we rode along a wide corridor in the spruce and pine forest. It was wider than Indians would cut for a wagon road. I had puzzled over this swath on my packhorse trips in 1933 and 1934. My curiosity about the history of the country had led me to an account of the Pacific and Hudson Bay Railway Company which intended to build a railway from Hudson Bay to Bella Coola. The wide trail was a railway right-of-way. The Great War had put a stop to the crackbrained scheme. As a consequence of some white men's industrial dreams, the Indians of Ulkatcho had a few miles of extra-wide trail. I tried to imagine them lining up at Ulkatcho to buy a train ticket to Bella Coola instead of saddling up for a three-day horse trip.

I shouted back to the end of our packtrain. "Joe, did you know that this part of the trail was made for a railway? Let's take the train to Ulkatcho."

"We take train to Ulkatcho—we take packtrain." He chuckled. He was pleased with his play on words in a foreign language. Joe had only the vaguest idea of what a railway train was. He had never seen one. The closest railway to Ulkatcho was two hundred miles north at Burns Lake or two hundred miles east at Quesnel.

At Ulkatcho Harold and I rode to the trading post to visit John Ward. "You aren't white men, are you?" exclaimed the trader. "I wish you would shave so I could get a good look at you. I haven't seen a white man since Father Thomas was here in June."

After a cup of tea we remounted and trotted over to the cabin where our packhorses stood. Joe Cahoose reluctantly left his wife at the cabin door.

A few hours ride north of Ulkatcho we camped beside the Entiako River. As soon as the packsaddles were off and the packhorses hobbled, Joe announced, "I go Ulkatcho. I come tomorrow."

"Okay, Joe," I said. "But get here early."

He jabbed his heels into his horse's ribs. In two hours he would be home with his wife.

Harold Giles inscribing names on a moose antler at the Tetachuck River.

At dawn a heavy rain began to beat on the tent. I went back to sleep. Some time later a voice woke me, "Hello, this camp." Joe was back.

"Come out of the rain, Joe," I shouted through the canvas.

He threw back the door flap. "We ride today?"

"After the rain stops. I can't take pictures in this weather."

The wet weather camped with us. Harold and I fretted—we were wasting time. Joe calmly ate a big breakfast and then picked out a spruce tree that did not leak. He wrapped himself in a canvas pack cover and slept all day under the tree. He was no longer in a hurry: it was not haying weather, and I was paying rent on his horses.

Joe was bright and full of jokes in the morning. Harold and I were sluggish and grouchy. The weather improved only in variety: the rain turned to sleet and hail.

We rode glumly through a forest that even in fine weather would offer few photographs.

On the third day after leaving Ulkatcho we broke out of the forest onto the bank of the Tetachuck River.

"Where does the trail go from here, Joe?" I asked.

He pointed to the far bank.

"A pretty wet-looking trail," I observed. "But if we have to swim the horses, we'd better do it this afternoon. Then we can spend the evening drying the outfit and get an early start tomorrow."

Harold had never swum horses before. Actually, neither had I, although I had done some pretty deep wading.

I turned to our horse wrangler. "Have you ever swum a river with horses, Joe?" He lacked the grin that usually sprang to his face when I spoke to him. He just shook his head and continued to gaze at the relentless current.

"Maybe I stop this place. You take pack off steamboat horse, make boat. I go Ulkatcho."

"No, Joe, we need your horses to carry our gear around Tetachuck Falls to the lake. I hired you to take us to Tetachuck Lake—all the way, not just part-way."

While Joe and I debated the river crossing, Harold went to a message tree on the river bank. Beneath the tree was a moose antler. "What message shall we leave?" he asked.

I suggested, "How about this? 'Joe Cahoose, Harold Giles and Cliff Kopas attempted a crossing on August 11, 1938.'"

"I don't like the phrase 'attempted a crossing'—it's too wordy. I'll just write 'crossed.'"

To our amazed eyes a boat containing four men drifted into view. Harold and I hollered in unison. Joe's face lit up with a relieved grin.

The man in the stern pulled on the starter cord of an outboard engine, and the other three reeled in their fishing lines.

The boatman cut the engine when Harold caught the bow at the water's edge. "You wouldn't want some help getting your gear across, would you?"

"We will pay for it," I volunteered enthusiastically.

"There's no charge. We were just drifting back to camp anyway."

"You are a gentleman and a scholar."

191

Our new friend was Billy McNeill, a guide who lived at Streatham on Ootsa Lake. He was guiding the three fishermen through the Big Circle chain of Tweedsmuir Park lakes. They were camped at Euchu Lake, just out of sight around a bend in the river.

The fishermen hopped out of the boat and watched us unload the packhorses.

"Three trips should see you and your gear across," said Billy McNeill. "What about the horses? One of you will have to ride ahead of the bunch to get them started."

I turned to Joe. "They are your horses, Joe."

The fishermen were excited by the prospect of watching five horses swim the river. Joe, Harold and I were apprehensive. Only Billy McNeill had much idea about what to expect. The previous year he had watched the string of horses for the governor-general's trip swim the Ootsa River. He told us that the horses had been swept far downstream, their heads just above the water. The cowboy who rode the leading horse had emerged from the river soaked but for his hat. He took a cigarette from his headpiece and lit it triumphally on the shore.

Billy McNeill explained that some horses are high swimmers and some are low swimmers. On a high swimmer the rider may get wet only to the waist; on a low swimmer he may have to dismount and hang onto the mane or tail to allow the horse to float higher. Being in the midst of a bunch of plunging, snorting horses is a hair-raising experience but it is less dangerous than letting go of your horse and striking out on your own.

I turned to Joe. "Harold has very little experience with horses. We can't expect him to take them across. That leaves you and me—and they are your horses."

Joe had been silent since the fishermen arrived. While the white men talked, he had been thinking.

Slowly and carefully for everyone to hear, he said, "Chief always brave man. Chief always go first."

Billy McNeill looked at me questioningly. "Does that settle it?"

"Yes, I suppose it does." My heart began to beat fast.

Joe and Harold pulled the saddles from their horses. I loosened the cinch a little on mine. I mounted.

"You fellows run the other horses in behind me when I'm out a ways," I ordered.

I nudged my horse into the river. When the water reached my horse's chest, there were whoops and hollers on the shore, and the smack of ropes on horses' rumps. I heard the splashing of hooves as the other four horses came up behind me. The water rose up my legs and onto the saddle.

I concentrated on the opposite shore. It did not seem to come any closer. My horse lost bottom and we floated. I was riding a high swimmer; even his withers were out of the water. I felt a great sense of exhilaration. I was on a floating island, drifting in marvellous freedom and silence, except for the puffing and snorting of the horses behind me.

In a few minutes my horse touched bottom and heaved out onto shore. The wonderful journey was over. I turned about and looked on the silent river, not with fear now but with triumph.

Billy McNeill brought Joe over with the first load of gear, then returned for Harold. "Well, Joe," I said, "you are dry, but I am a great chief."

He replied, "I always say you chief. Fight yellowjacket, buck off horse, swim river. Skookum tumtum."

Joe was an accomplished flatterer. I reminded myself that in a few hours I would be paying him—and I was obliged to pay for his services, not for his flattery.

Billy McNeill delivered Harold and the rest of the outfit. Before leaving he promised to take Joe back across the river in the morning.

"You are a lucky Indian," I told our Ulkatcho outfitter.

He grinned. "I know why white man white: he go in water lotsa time. Indian he stay outa water: he stay brown."

"It's an interesting theory," I said. "Even plausible if Joe Cahoose is any example."

We packed the horses again and rode up the ridge above Tetachuck Falls. The river roared and tumbled white over a twenty-foot drop.

In a couple of hours we broke out of the forest onto the shore of Tetachuck Lake. We unpacked the horses on the beach. Joe wanted to see the *Lily* in the water before he left, so we put him to work assembling the craft. He laid the rubberized canvas on the ground and then fastened a series of wire ribs to loops at the gunwales. The resulting structure resembled a canoe and looked even more so with the addition of a seat and oarlocks. The *Lily* did not have good lines but she had plenty of them.

"Now for the launching ceremony," I said.

"Or scuttling ceremony," amended Harold. He clearly was not as impressed with the *Lily* as I was.

"Bring the champagne, Joe," I said. The Indian gave me a blank look; champagne and launching ceremonies were not part of his experience. Nor mine, either, if the truth be told, but I read more widely.

Harold and I each took an end of the *Lily* and waded into Tetachuck Lake. We gingerly set the boat on the water. It floated like a bubble.

"It won't leak sitting on top like that," I said. "For a true test it needs a load. I'll hold it steady while you get in."

Harold placed a foot in the centre of the boat and carefully shifted his weight onto it. The craft sank slightly.

"It floats higher than I imagined it would," I said admiringly. "Are there any leaks?"

"The canvas is sweating, that's all."

"That will stop as soon as the fibres swell," I said confidently. "Now that you are aboard, Harold, you might as well give the engine a try." I turned to Joe who was standing with the toes of his boots in the lake. "Bring the oars and oarlocks, Joe. Let's see how much horsepower the *Lily* can produce."

Harold rowed into the lake slowly at first, then briskly. He pulled hard at the oars, and one of them popped out of an oarlock. By this time the boat was at the outlet of the lake. The gentle current caught the craft. *Lily* drifted sideways down the first riffle.

Joe
Cahoose
assembling
the
rubberized
canvas
canoe
known as
Lily.

I was in bare feet. I looked on helplessly. Joe sprinted down the lakeshore at a good clip for someone in cowboy boots. Harold got the oarlock back in place and was heading for shore before he was in danger of going over Tetachuck Falls. Joe Cahoose stayed ready for action but dry.

In the morning Harold and I plied Joe with hotcakes and syrup. Harold's analytical mind had Joe's nutritional needs figured out. "It's forty miles to Ulkatcho, Joe. Each hotcake is good for two miles. You need twenty hotcakes plus one for the river crossing."

"Too heavy for get into saddle pretty soon," protested Joe.

"Never mind, Cliff and I will boost you up."

Harold and I rode back to the river crossing with Joe to await

195

Billy McNeill and his boat. We unsaddled all the horses.

Billy arrived with his fishermen; the fishermen wanted to see the spectacle of horses swimming the Tetachuck River again.

We loaded the saddles into the boat. Then, with much hollering and arm-waving, we chased the horses into the river. Joe stepped into the bow of the boat, and Harold pushed it from the shore. "Sorry to see you go, Joe," I shouted above the sputter of the outboard engine. "But you and your horses would overload our canoe."

We watched the horses and the men in the boat gain the far shore. "I hope your calculation about the hotcakes is correct," I told Harold. "Joe is certain to try to ride forty miles to get home today. That is about the limit for man and horse in this country."

"He will do it. There is nothing more difficult than to keep a newly married guy in the bush away from his wife."

"Unless he is broke," I said pointedly.

We walked back up the trail to Tetachuck Lake. At camp Harold said hesitantly, "I guess we'd better eat lunch before we load the boat."

"Yes, I suppose we had better."

Neither of us would admit it but we were reluctant to launch forth onto the large wilderness lakes in a written-off canvas boat. We did not know what to expect of the lakes, the boat, the weather or ourselves.

While we ate lunch we discussed procedure. I said, "The old fur traders never ran their birchbark canoes onto the beach. They treated the boats with great care. We must do the same. We will load and unload in the water. If we rip the canvas, we will be sunk in more ways than one."

Harold said, "I will load the boat. I will even load you into it so that you won't have to get wet." He seemed incredibly magnanimous.

"I am glad you listened carefully to Joe Cahoose and learned that I am truly the chief. The Chief Factor of the Hudson's Bay Company used to be carried into his canoe too."

Harold looked at me steadily. "Cliff, I really am not concerned about your wet feet. I just don't want you capsizing the boat while clambering in and out. As for the chief stuff, the *Lily* is too small for a chief officer. She is too small for any officer. All she can accommodate is freight and working parts. The working parts are you and me. I am the engine; you are the bailing pump."

Evidently, with Joe Cahoose gone, Harold Giles had taken over the direction of my trip.

Harold loaded the front half of the canvas boat with our gear. The bow sank deep into the water and the stern jutted out. "I'll lift you into her now to put her on an even keel," Harold said. He picked me up and strode into the water. With me in his arms, he could not see where he was placing his feet. He put a bare foot on a sharp, loose rock. He winced, stumbled, almost regained his balance, then fell over backward with me on top of him. Struggling to get up, I pushed Harold completely under. Finally we both found bottom and struck for shore.

"That was a good idea about keeping me dry for the boat," I said.

"There is always some disharmony between theory and practice at the initiation of a new enterprise," Harold replied loftily.

While we were collecting wood for a fire to dry our clothes, rain began to fall. What luck! We now had an excuse to postpone casting off onto the big, unknown lakes.

"We should try to keep our gear dry," I said uncertainly.

Without hesitation, Harold agreed. "Yes, I'll take it out of the canoe."

In a few minutes we had our tent up again and our gear inside. We were excellent campers.

"It looks like we are here for another night," I said cheerily.

"We should take the canoe out of the lake," said Harold.

We untied the bow line from its tree, waded to the boat and lifted it ashore.

"The Hudson's Bay men turned their canoes upside down beside their camp," I explained.

We turned *Lily* upside down and the seat fell out, causing the entire craft to collapse like a deflated snake. Harold viewed the scene of destruction and commented, "She certainly is carefully engineered."

We reconstructed the boat and left it right side up.

Rain pelted most of the night, but at dawn the sun glittered through droplets on twigs and needles and brilliantly outlined the spruce trees east of camp.

Harold crawled out of the tent and inspected *Lily*. The bottom of the canoe was inches deep in rainwater. "Good news, Cliff," Harold announced. "The boat holds water. If it holds it in, it will hold it out." He continued with a weather report. "It's foggy but calm. Let's start out before a wind comes up."

I joined Harold beside the *Lily*. "If we skip breakfast we will save more than an hour," I suggested. Apprehension about setting forth on the lake in an overloaded canoe had taken my appetite. "I'll get the bailing can and practise my new occupation with this rainwater."

We struck the tent and then carried the canoe to the lake. I took our gear to the water's edge, and Harold deposited it in the boat. Finally he lifted me into the stern. Then, with a careful hop, he landed on the seat in the centre of the craft and took up the oars.

I looked over the gunwale. We had six inches of freeboard. "I believe we will be obliged to be fair weather sailors," I said.

"Fair weather sailors—and never more than an oar's length from shore," Harold agreed.

I watched globules of water appear on the canvas hull, grow and trickle to the bottom of the boat.

"The canvas is weeping," I said.

"It's sweating," said Harold.

Harold rowed steadily, and I bailed intermittently. Our wake parallelled the bays and points of the shoreline. Fog licked at the surface of the lake at first, then rose a little. The far shore peeked under the white curtain, ending the illusion that the lake was limitless. Sailing in the fog above us, the sun was a silver dollar without King George's face.

The fog fled from the sun. The chill left the air. The country became smaller now that we could see it—and friendlier too. Hills and forests danced on their heads in the *Lily's* wake.

As we became familiar with the lake and the capabilities of our craft, our courage mounted. We began to leave the security of the shore, first risking direct routes from point to point, and eventually rowing out into the lake to inspect islands. Finally we abandoned our fears and accepted the freedom of the lake that our boat gave us.

Late in the second day we reached the end of Tetachuck Lake and the mouth of a short river that came down from Eutsuk Lake. The river was little more than a mile long but it was bigger than the Bella Coola River and nearly as swift.

We dismantled the *Lily* and carried her up the bushy portage trail to the shore of Eutsuk Lake.

Just as we arrived back at the Tetachuck Lake end of the portage for our final load, a deer stepped out of the trees onto the beach. It was close to us and unafraid.

"There you are, Harold," I said. "We need the grub. The rifle is on your pack."

Harold was tired and sweaty. "I'm not killing anything I have to carry over the portage," he asserted. "You herd it up the trail; I'll shoot it at the other end."

"I've never known deer to herd well," I said. I stepped toward the animal; it sprang into the forest.

As we stumbled up the portage trail for the last time, a wind swept through the narrow valley. Trees bent under it. Billy McNeill had told us about Eutsuk Lake. It was beautiful; it was treacherous; its winds began suddenly and blew for days.

We set up camp at the outlet of the lake. Our tent billowed like a sail. Whitecaps marched down the lake and stumbled onto the beach.

"It's just an afternoon westerly coming over the mountains from the ocean," I explained to Harold confidently. Being a schoolteacher from the city, he did not have an opinion on the matter. It turned out that his lack of opinion was closer to the truth than my certain knowledge.

The wind did not abate in the evening, nor during the night, nor the next day. We dared not venture onto the lake. Our strength and freeboard were no match for the wind and waves of Big Eutsuk.

To pass the time, we tipped the *Lily* upside down on the beach and spread pine tar on her bottom.

"I wonder if the canvas will overheat if it stops sweating," mused Harold.

"Considering the terrific speed at which we travel, it undoubtedly will," I said. "I'm impressed with your oarsmanship. Do you realize that you and *Lily* are doing the work of two packhorses and two saddlehorses, and travelling farther in a day?" I had learned from Joe Cahoose that judicious flattery could bring great rewards and feared that Harold was going to suggest that I take a turn at the oars.

Instead Harold said humbly, "Packhorses don't stop for wind."

We stared moodily at the waves. How long would the wind last? We were its captives. While it blew we could neither go up Eutsuk Lake nor back down Tetachuck Lake. We could only sit and slowly consume our grub.

Next morning the wind slacked off a little, or perhaps it was only our fervent yearning that made it seem so. Whitecaps still streamed down the lake.

We balanced the load carefully in the canoe and set forth. The wind immediately threw a couple of fierce gusts at us. Harold pulled hard on the oars to get away from the shore.

To our surprise the *Lily* rode the waves well; her sides pulsated like a panting toad. She took the waves particularly well on her beam. They seemed to slip quietly under her round belly.

But we could not travel continuously beam-to because the wind pushed us ashore. To get away from the land we had to take the waves head-on. Each time the bow rose on a large wave I had to shift my weight forward almost onto Harold's lap. Otherwise the stern dipped under the water and, as sailors say, the craft was pooped.

For several hours we struggled along the rocky coast. The wind pushed us persistently toward it. From time to time we had to head out to deeper water away from the land. Whenever we were going directly into the waves, I informed Harold about especially large ones coming. He would then turn the canoe broadside to allow them to sweep underneath. We crabbed along like this, not making much headway. Besides observing the swells, constantly shifting my weight to compensate for the rising and falling bow, and bailing water that poured over the stern, I kept an eye peeled for a place to land. The low, sullen bluffs seemed to rebuff us silently for being audacious fools.

Eventually a landing place appeared, more a patch of boulders than a beach. We let the wind push us toward it. In shallow water Harold hopped out and guided the boat among the boulders. A succession of waves spilled over the stern. It didn't matter any more; we were safe.

For two days we waited. For two days the wind blew, and waves dashed themselves onto the boulders. We waited and ate beans. It was too windy and rough even for fishing.

On the third day I awoke at dawn. Except for Harold's snoring there was no sound.

"Harold!" I whooped.

He shot up in his sleeping bag. "Whatsa matter?"

"Listen," I said. There was a moment of silence.

"What's the matter with you? I don't hear a thing."

"That's the point!" I exclaimed. "There's no wind!"

Under the gaze of the morning star we packed our gear onto the *Lily*. At five o'clock the oars dug into the surface of Eutsuk Lake and began their rhythmical creak. Twin swirls of water six feet apart in a long succession behind us measured our pace.

"How shall we travel today?" asked Harold. "Shall we creep along the shore or go from point to point?"

The cold morning and lack of breakfast made me averse to deciding anything. I turned the question back, "Why come down into the bowels of the ship to put navigational problems to the bailer?"

"Okay, then. It will be point to point. The engine gets more miles per bean that way and it's low on fuel."

Harold was in a good frame of mind. Rowing warmed and invigorated him, dispelling the lethargy that had descended on us while we were trapped by the wind.

At nine o'clock we brought the *Lily* to a stop at a sandy beach. It was breakfast time. Strangely I was the one overwhelmed by hunger. Harold, who was doing the work, was not hungry. He wanted to row and row and row. The rhythm of it seemed to put him into a sort of trance.

"You will collapse when your last bean is digested," I warned him.

"It is apparent from the smell of the exhaust that the beans are not used up yet," he replied.

We cooked rolled oats for breakfast. Then we launched again onto the unruffled lake. It was like crossing an immense mirror that reflected mushrooming clouds.

Ahead, to our right, a moving black object appeared.

"Moving object off the starboard bow," I reported briskly. "We are on a collision course."

Harold smiled indulgently, "It will fly in a moment."

"It doesn't look like a bird," I said. "Stay on course and we'll cut across its path—whatever it is."

As our paths closed I made out short, round ears on the swimming object. A snuffling sound crossed the surface of the water. "It's a black bear," I announced. "Let's get close enough for a picture."

We approached slowly, and the bear slowed too. It breathed heavily, its nose expanding and contracting. It turned its dark, shiny eyes toward us beseechingly.

"It looks afraid," I said.

I was wrong. The animal began to swim toward us.

"He wants to come aboard!" I exclaimed. "Let's get out of here."

Harold dug the oars into the lake. The *Lily* made a fat-bellied move forward, not fast but with momentum. In a few minutes she had a modest bow wave. The canvas hull pulsated at each pull on the oars.

"We are not very neighbourly," I pointed out to Harold when we were far enough away from the bear to be nonchalant.

"This boat does not pick up passengers, particularly passengers with claws," Harold pronounced firmly.

In the evening we spotted a log cabin tucked in the trees above a lagoon. We went ashore and inspected the building. It had a stove, table, chairs and bunks. A note on the door welcomed visitors if they kept the cabin clean and cut their own firewood.

Immediately after supper we chose our bunks. The long day in the bright sun had drained our energy. In the cabin, undisturbed by mosquitoes, we slept with a soundness rarely achieved outdoors.

The sighing of wind in the trees awoke me. I pushed open the door to look at the lake. The lagoon was calm except for cat's paws. Farther out, whitecaps winked.

I awoke Harold to get his opinion on the weather.

"I don't like it much," he said. "But we have to travel more than one day in four or we will run out of grub."

We launched the *Lily* just as the sun reached over the cottonwood trees that bordered the lagoon. For several miles we crept beneath high cliffs that blunted the force of the wind. When the land flattened out, the wind picked up.

Suddenly the seat under Harold broke. In a boat constructed so that every part depended on every other part for support, the collapse of the seat pulled the oarlock sockets out of position.

Harold sat dumbfounded on the bottom of the boat for a moment, then said quietly, "We're helpless."

The boat swung broadside to the weather, the position in which she took it best. Waves stopped slopping aboard.

"We have to paddle ashore," I said. I took one oar and Harold took the other. He knelt on the broken seat, facing forward. Keeping the canoe broadside to the waves, we paddled across the bay we were in. Near shore Harold stepped out of the canoe and guided it among

Harold Giles lifting the portage railcar back onto its tracks on the quarter-mile portage between Eutsuk Lake and Whitesail Lake.

boulders to land. Once again we were safe but stranded.

With a familiar feeling of imprisonment, we unloaded our gear among the boulders. Harold went to work on the broken seat. I took the rifle and headed into the bush in search of grouse. When I returned—without grouse—the canoe was ready for use. But the lake wasn't.

We had become obsessed with trying to interpret portents of weather. We analyzed and discussed every streamer of cirrus, every billow of cumulus. We surveyed the height and vivacity of whitecaps. Most of all we calculated the speed of the wind, listened to its sounds and tried to predict its changes.

We went to bed with the sound of wind in the trees and waves on the boulders.

At the peep of dawn I awoke to the sound only of rain on the tent roof.

"Daylight in the swamp, Harold," I said loudly. "Time to sail."

Harold muttered, "It's still dark. What time is it?"

"Five o'clock. Who cares? There's no wind."

The portage rail terminus at Whitesail Lake.

The lake whispered under the rain. Except for drop-dimples it was smooth. We were on it by five-thirty.

"I believe the way to avoid the wind is to sneak out under cover of darkness," said Harold. It was his hundredth theory about wind and weather.

The surface of the lake remained a mirror all day. The clouds lifted. We were tempted north and south: on the south to explore inlets that led to the Coast Mountains; on the north to walk golden beaches.

In the afternoon we turned north into St. Thomas Bay, rounding a rust-coloured point on which the trees leaned at a forty-five degree angle. They indicated a strong, persistent wind from the west. I pointed to the trees. Harold nodded knowingly. We were lucky this day.

We coasted up to a small dock at the north end of St. Thomas Bay. From the dock a pair of iron rails led into the woods.

"A railway without a train," I remarked.

"The railcar must be at the other terminal," said Harold.

We followed the tracks a quarter of a mile through the woods to Chikamin Bay on Whitesail Lake. On a wharf like the one at Eutsuk Lake sat a small homemade flatcar with iron wheels.

"Do you think our boat engine can power a locomotive?" I asked Harold.

"Of course," he replied. "Even a boat bailer could be adapted for the job."

We each took a corner of the railcar, straddled a rail and began the long push back up the hill to Eutsuk Lake. The difference in elevation between Whitesail Lake and Eutsuk Lake was a hundred and twenty feet, and some pitches were steep. The rails were not absolutely parallel. Three times the railcar dropped off the tracks. We were soaked with sweat by the time we reached the jetty at Eutsuk Lake.

We loaded the *Lily* onto the railcar and started north on the Whitesail Lake Express.

"If the car gets away from us the canoe will launch itself into Whitesail Lake without our help," I said.

"There would be a derailment long before it got there," Harold asserted.

"And the result would be a dead *Lily*. If she shoots off the railway into the trees, she will be torn to shreds."

"Why doesn't the bailer become a brakeman?"

It was a good suggestion. I found a dry poplar pole to place ahead of the front wheels whenever the railcar picked up speed. We had two derailments on the way to Whitesail Lake, but at low speed.

We set up camp above the beach near the Whitesail wharf. As we relaxed beside the campfire after supper, I told Harold, "You did quite well today. You rowed thirty miles and handled five derailments. But I think it's time you considered doing a full day's work."

"Tomorrow," promised Harold without conviction and staggered off to bed.

The new day looked auspicious. Not a breath of air disturbed the surface of Whitesail Lake. Far above, feathery cirrus scarcely seemed to move.

We launched the canoe and headed straight down the middle of the lake a good distance from shore. I was enraptured by the scenery. "Another perfect day in the wilderness paradise of Tweedsmuir Park," I announced.

Harold stopped rowing. "I hear something," he said.

"It's called silence," I replied. "I've been hearing it all morning. I think it is the sound of time slipping by."

"Just listen!" Harold ordered.

I heard a moan, a dull roar, coming from Chikamin Mountain west of us. My heart leapt to my throat.

"It's the wind again!" I cried.

Harold dug the right oar into the water to turn the bow. Then he pulled on both oars with such force that the canoe's sides heaved.

The roar rose in pitch as the wind got nearer.

We were close to shore when the first gust hit us. But we dared not land among the boulders. We moved with the wind, parallel to the shoreline, looking for a place to go in. The wind soon licked the water into waves that curled over our low stern. I bailed furiously.

A small space appeared between the boulders. I pointed it out to Harold. "We have to try to get in there!" I chattered excitedly. "We're going to sink anyway. I can't keep ahead of the waves any more!"

Harold turned the bow toward shore once again and rowed toward the gap in the boulders. In shallow water the waves rose even higher. Harold shipped the oars and hopped overboard, nearly capsizing the canoe. The stern immediately sank below the waves. Up to my waist in water, I half-crawled, half-floated out of the boat. Harold pulled the foundering craft ashore while I stumbled along behind, clinging to the stern.

We sat a moment on the rocks to recover from our fright. Harold intoned, "Here we are in the wilderness paradise of Tweedsmuir Park with three wet bottoms and no place to pitch a tent."

A steep hillside rose above us. It supported a few scraggly pines that might serve as firewood. In any case we could not light a fire in the strong wind.

The wind howled down the lake all day. In the evening Harold and I spread our tent over the smallest boulders for a mattress. We settled ourselves into our sleeping bags among the humps and hollows. Throughout the night every move we made brought us awake.

The wind abated overnight. Squinting in the rising sun, we packed the canoe. We did not take time for breakfast. We had decided to eat in the wind and travel in the calm. We put a jam tin full of large white lima beans to soak in the bow, to be ready for our next windy meal.

We might as well have eaten breakfast; the wind did not blow all day.

We glided down the narrowing lake, passed several islands and

Harold Giles and Cliff Kopas in the *Lily* on the Whitesail River.

were drawn into a strong current. Whitesail River poured out of Whitesail Lake through a corridor lined with spruce trees.

We stayed close to the river bank, believing that to be the safest course. We were continually struggling to free ourselves from eddies that pushed us back up the river or swung us in circles.

"I can't control the canoe in this current," Harold admitted. "What would we do if we came to a sweeper jutting out from the bank?" He answered his own question, "We would be carried right under it."

"It's the middle of the river for us, I suppose," I said hesitantly. The river frightened me. On the lake the waves subsided with the wind, but the river current was relentless. On the lake patience could outwait danger, but on the river only boldness would do.

In the middle of the river we moved swiftly and smoothly. There was great power in the current, yet it was gentle. Gradually we relaxed and enjoyed our quick, effortless passage through the wilderness.

We approached a bend in the river. Above the slack water on the inside curve stood a couple of tents and a fly over a table. A man arose from the table and ran down to the river's edge.

"Come on in," he shouted. "The coffee pot is on."

Harold took up the oars and rowed to shore. As our canoe approached the beach, the man grasped the bow with one hand. With the other he wiped his eyes in a gesture of disbelief.

"I've seen outfits like yours go into the wilderness," he said. "This is the first one I've seen come out. Usually we just take some names off the voters' list."

We lifted the *Lily* onto the sand and followed Cliff Harrison to his camp, where we met his two brothers Buster and Orald, his two young sons and three schoolteachers.

"We are showing the young ladies around the lakes a bit before they tackle our kids in the schoolroom," Cliff explained. "You guys are the strangest sight they've seen yet. They thought you were drifting down the middle of the river without a boat. They'd heard of people walking on water; sitting on it was a new wrinkle."

The Harrisons were waiting for their thirty-five-foot launch, the *Lady Tweedsmuir*, to return them to Ootsa Lake. "I insist that you fellows come with us," Cliff said. "You have been so lucky and brave I have to admire you. But I don't want you drowning on my doorstep. It might spoil the fishing."

Cliff Harrison began to tell me about how his parents, who were pioneers at Ootsa Lake, had reached the country by coming over the trail from Bella Coola thirty-one years earlier. I began to take notes for a magazine story about Ootsa Lake pioneers.

Harold interrupted us, "Before you get too busy, could you help me put the canoe in the water. I've invited one of the girls out for a ride." He turned to Cliff Harrison. "I hope it's all right if your son comes along too."

I looked at Harold seriously. "You don't need a chaperone. We trust you to behave yourself. In the *Lily* you have to behave yourself or you capsize."

"The boy is for balance," Harold responded testily. "I'm taking the lady out because of mutual academic interests."

We went down the beach to the canoe. Harold had already dumped our lima beans into the river. They gleamed below the surface. Cliff Harrison looked intently at them for a moment, then exclaimed, "First clams I've seen so far from salt water."

A few minutes later we heard an airplane approaching. I looked into the sky. I couldn't see a thing.

"There she is, coming around the bend!" Cliff Harrison shouted proudly. I took my eyes from the sky and looked down the river. A cabin cruiser powered by a car engine and an airplane propeller sped toward us.

The Harrisons had been building their cabin cruiser when Lord and Lady Tweedsmuir visited Ootsa Lake. They received vice-regal permission to name their boat the *Lady Tweedsmuir*.

Harold and I dismantled the *Lily* while the Harrisons and the schoolteachers took down their camp. The *Lily*, once again an awkward bundle, was put aboard the *Lady Tweedsmuir*. I felt a twinge of regret to see our brave boat reduced to baggage.

210

We roared down the Whitesail River and out onto Ootsa Lake at an alarming speed. We pulled ashore at Wistaria (named after one of Mrs. Harrison's garden plants) where the Harrisons owned pre-empted land.

The family was tremendously hospitable. When they heard that I wanted to photograph the lakes of Tweedsmuir Park, Orald Harrison and his wife offered to take Harold and me on a boat trip through the east end of the Great Circle of Lakes. We loaded a twenty-foot lake boat with gear and grub for a four-day journey. Harrison's nanny goat, who loved to travel by boat, wanted to come. Orald told her she had to stay behind; it was punishment for eating a sweater. He told us her odour attracted bears into camp.

Pushed by a sixteen horsepower outboard engine, we cruised the length of Ootsa Lake and then descended Joan Rapids and Pope

The *Lady Tweedsmuir* on the Whitesail River.

Orald Harrison and Cliff Kopas with a grizzly bear hide.

Rapids. Orald handled his boat with the same degree of skill that Joe Cahoose had shown handling his horses on the first part of our trip.

"Where there is competence there is no adventure," I pointed out to Harold.

We camped at Point Susan (named after Lady Tweedsmuir) on beautiful Intata Lake where the vice-regal party had stayed a year earlier. I asked Orald for names of other points, bays and mountains. "I don't think they have names," he said. "This country is too big to name."

Next morning we entered lovely Natalkuz Lake, the easternmost lake in the Great Circle. The Nechako River flowed east from it and out of Tweedsmuir Park. We turned abruptly west around Jim Smith Point and headed for Euchu Lake.

Late in the afternoon we left Euchu Lake and ascended the Tetachuck River. Harold and I recognized the trail crossing place at the same time. "There it is!" we called out in unison.

212

Orald told us, "The oldtimers at Ootsa Lake call the trail to Bella Coola the Three Swims Trail. They had to swim their horses across the Ootsa River, the Tetachuck River and the Bella Coola River. At the Bella Coola end there was an Indian dugout canoe attached to a cable to ferry freight across. At this end the freight had to be taken across the Tetachuck and Ootsa on rafts."

"For me it was the One Swim Trail," I said. "And one swim was enough."

Harold and I had completed the circuit of the big lakes of Tweedsmuir Park, the Great Circle, a distance of over two hundred miles. We camped for the night within earshot of Tetachuck Falls where we had started.

Two days later we cruised back along Ootsa Lake. Orald Harrison called out the names of the owners of the homesteads as we passed them. Each homestead was marked by a cluster of log cabins and a boat or two drawn up on the beach.

At the settlement of Ootsa Landing, Orald set us ashore at Schreiber's Store. "You will have lots to talk to him about," he said. "Norman Schreiber has been here about twenty years—spent his first winter in a tent. He used to canoe around the circle of lakes trading for furs with the Indians. After he got married he settled down to delivering mail and keeping store. He is due to leave for Burns Lake tomorrow on his regular run. He'll give you a ride."

In the morning Harold and I waited on the porch of Schreiber's Store. The Quanchus Mountains were reflected perfectly on the calm surface of Ootsa Lake. It would have been an ideal day for canoeing.

"This place is enough to incite me to poetry," I said.

"Give it a try," said Harold.

I scribbled for a few minutes and then handed my notebook to Harold. He read haltingly:

"We tripped so cheerily through Tweedsmuir Park
With five fine horses and a collapsible barque.
We travelled by light and camped in the dark
And had a wonderful time on our watery lark."

Harold looked up with a pleased smile. "That sums it up in

heroic couplets," he said approvingly.

Norman Schreiber stopped his truck in front of his store. He went inside to get the mail for Burns Lake while Harold and I tossed our baggage into the truck, leaving the canvas boat bundle to the last.

"Let's leave it here for the local kids," I suggested. "It's not worth the freight charges between here and Bella Coola."

Harold, looking pensive, did not reply. Only Schreiber's truck had anything to say; it chugged contentedly in neutral.

Eventually Harold said slowly, "I'd hate to abandon her. She did us well."

My initial reaction was annoyance. The boat was no more than an assemblage of metal rods, strips of wood and rubberized canvas designed to obey Archimedes' principle when arranged in a particular way. It had served its purpose. Harold's sentimentality seemed to indicate that too much time in the bush damages sensitive personalities, or perhaps that his normal good sense had been swept away by my poetry.

While we hesitated, I felt a disconcerting return of the twinge of regret I'd had when I saw the *Lily* loaded onto the *Lady Tweedsmuir*.

"Okay, let's take her with us," I said finally. "She still has another trip in her."

We lifted the *Lily* bundle onto the back of the truck.

Afterword

My father Cliff Kopas was twenty-seven years old when he travelled by horse and boat through the new Tweedsmuir Park. I was pretty new myself: six weeks. I stayed back at Bella Coola with my mother. Evidently my father's pursuit of adventure had too much impetus to be stopped just because I had arrived. I slowed him down, though.

My father knew—but found hard to accept—that he could not support a family on the meagre returns of a writer. While my mother Mae Kopas worked as a nurse at the Bella Coola Hospital, he built an addition to their two-room shack. The sign on the addition read:

C. R. KOPAS

PHOTOGRAPHIC AND GIFT SHOP

The idea behind the sign must have seemed preposterous in a community as small as Bella Coola, but today the Cliff Kopas store is nearly sixty, the oldest business in the valley.

Cliff Kopas continued to take packhorses into the mountains, particularly his beloved Rainbows. The journeys were shorter than before, and geared to photography rather than adventure. Mae accompanied him as cook and photographic human interest. As youthfulness faded and fortune grew, Cliff Kopas hired guides—always Ulkatcho Indians—to do the horse wrangling and packing.

Sometimes he and Clayton Mack went bear hunting at Kwatna Inlet west of Bella Coola, Clayton's rifle backing up Cliff's camera. One time, the renowned anthropologist Thor Heyerdahl (he was not renowned then) went with them.

At Kwatna, Cliff Kopas met Alex Sahonovitch, a handlogger his age, a son of the resident Polish stump farmers. A few years later,

Alex was badly injured. In a desperate attempt to earn a living, he taught himself the printing trade and in 1945 launched the *Cariboo Digest* magazine in Quesnel. From the first, my father wrote articles for Sahonovitch's magazine, and the last article he ever wrote was published in the *Digest* in 1979. It was about the Bella Coola road. In 1995 the magazine (now called *BC Outdoors*) celebrated its fiftieth anniversary, the oldest continuously published British Columbia magazine.

Two interests occupied the attention of Cliff Kopas for most of his years in Bella Coola: The Road and The Book. The Road had been a Bella Coola obsession ever since Norwegian settlers arrived in 1894. By the time my father exchanged packhorsing for community activities, the gravel road through the valley—grandly called the Mackenzie Highway—extended to Mosher Creek fifty miles from the ocean. The rest of the provincial highway system stopped at Anahim Lake. There was a frustrating gap of forty miles.

Cliff Kopas became the publicist for The Road. About 1950 he

Mae Kopas at Mae Lake on the rim of the Bella Coola Valley.

went to Vancouver to attend a conference on highways and listened to delegates complain about potholes everywhere. When he took his turn at the podium he proposed that everyone throughout the province should send their potholes to Bella Coola, and the local citizens would put them end-to-end to Anahim Lake. He returned home with a five-pound pothole and the title King of the Potholes—but no promises from the government. In 1952 the people of Bella Coola told the government that they were going to build the road themselves, and they did. For Cliff Kopas the joy of success was balanced by disappointment: the *Saturday Evening Post* almost accepted his article about the building of The Road. Big-time journalism had just eluded him.

The Book grew from my father's love of local history. He collected information about Bella Coola wherever he could find it. The Book, published in 1970, was called *Bella Coola: A Story of Effort and Achievement.*

Another book, the first draft of which had been written in a shack in lower Bella Coola in 1934, was published in 1976 with the

The Chimney Creek Bridge across the Fraser River.

title *Packhorses to the Pacific*. It told the story of the packhorse journey of Cliff and Ruth Kopas from Alberta to Bella Coola.

My father wrote the stories in this book shortly before his time ran out in 1978. It always took a long time to get his books published, and this book upholds the tradition. In any case, there was no need to hurry. It is not a guidebook. The journeys recounted here cannot be repeated, and the country has changed. Young people can no longer roam the southern Rockies on horseback without constraint. The great circle of lakes in northern Tweedsmuir Park is now largely a snag-ridden industrial reservoir. Missionary doctors do not visit patients on horseback nowadays. The Telegraph Trail is abandoned because telegraph is abandoned. The Canoe Crossing Trail, the Burnt Bridge Trail and the Tweedsmuir Trail disappeared under downed trees and bushes after The Road was built.

The wheel of time is turning things right. Recently the government has begun to return Tweedsmuir Park to the way it was when Cliff Kopas knew it. Old horse trails have been cleared. A start has been made to clear the snags from the Nechako Reservoir. At Tanya Lakes, the Ulkatcho Indians have built a new smokehouse, the first in many years. The land is not much changed from the old days, and it still has the worst mosquitoes in Canada.

Index